WRITING YOUR FAMILY HISTORY

A Guide for Family Historians

Gill Blanchard

Pen & Sword
FAMILY HISTORY

First published in Great Britain in 2014 by
PEN & SWORD FAMILY HISTORY
an imprint of
Pen & Sword Books Ltd
47 Church Street
Barnsley
South Yorkshire
S70 2AS

ISBN 978 1 78159 372 1

Typeset in Palatino and Optima by
CHIC GRAPHICS

Printed and bound in England by
CPI Group (UK), Croydon, CR0 4YY

Pen & Sword Books Ltd incorporates the imprints of Pen & Sword
Archaeology, Atlas, Aviation, Battleground, Discovery, Family History, History,
Maritime, Military, Naval, Politics, Railways, Select, Social History, Transport,
True Crime, and Claymore Press, Frontline Books, Leo Cooper, Praetorian
Press, Remember When, Seaforth Publishing and Wharncliffe.

For a complete list of Pen & Sword titles please contact
PEN & SWORD BOOKS LTD
47 Church Street, Barnsley, South Yorkshire, S70 2AS, England
E-mail: enquiries@pen-and-sword.co.uk
Website: www.pen-and-sword.co.uk

WRITING R
FAMILY
HISTORY

FAMILY HISTORY FROM PEN & SWORD

CONTENTS

ACKNOWLEDGEMENTS

To my personal editorial and proofreading team Cáitlin Blanchard, Ian Buckingham and Ellinor Orton. Any mistakes that remain after their efforts are, of course, all mine. As storytellers and writers in their own right Cáitlin and Ellinor provided much appreciated feedback on the content. Additional thanks must also go to fellow author and genealogist Simon Fowler for being a 'fierce friend'.

Cáitlin Blanchard, Ian Buckingham and Alex Orton are the source of most of the technical advice on websites and blogs. The cartoons in this book were specially created for me by Sascha Stiven, and are her copyright (her website is www.sascha-stiven.co.uk).

Stories about my family and folk songs and tales of the past have been the inspiration for much of my own writing. This book is for storytellers everywhere, whether in words, music or song. Your family history is your story. It is time to tell the tale.

INTRODUCTION

Who, What, Where, When, Why and How?

As family historians, the questions 'who, what, where, when, why and how' underpin the quest to find out about our ancestors. Who they were; what they did; where they came from or went to; when key events in their lives occurred; why and how they made certain decisions, and so on. These are the fundamental questions or themes that lie underneath every story, whether fact or fiction. This book aims to give you the tools to present the answers to those questions by telling the story of your ancestors' lives in an accessible and interesting manner.

Writing a family history is one of the best means to preserve and share your research with others both in the present and future. Whereas a family tree and research data are not necessarily things others can follow easily or feel connected to. Moreover, writing an ancestral story creates the opportunity to explore social history and places associated with your ancestry that may not have been pursued so far. In addition to which, reviewing and distilling the mass of information gathered to create a story is one of the best means I know of spotting gaps and anomalies and identifying what still needs to be checked.

My own interest in stories of the past originated with folk music. Songs, folk tales and legends of people's lives and historical events were my first experience of social and local history. Even their contradictions and anomalies helped to shape my view that history is all about people and the telling of their stories. I began to write family histories and then to teach others after developing my own writing skills through creative writing courses, writing guides and belonging to writers' and reading groups. For this book I have drawn on my own experiences of teaching and writing family histories professionally and for myself and family.

A desire to get to know our ancestors personally inevitably leads us to explore the social and historical context of their lives. Writing about those lives is one of the most creative methods by which we can explore the past and share it with others. Whether you are planning a full-length book, a short article for a family history magazine, a website or blog, writing a family history takes some work and discipline, but is immensely rewarding.

This book looks at the whole process of writing your family's history, including how to deal with practical problems and what you can do to make your writing more enjoyable and interesting. It assumes you already have a body of research to work from even if you have not completed all your research. There is a strong focus on how to write for a non-genealogical audience with plenty of practical advice, exercises and examples of writing.

When I began writing family histories I soon realised that genealogists had particular writing problems that most other writers do not experience. Whilst writers of biography and history (the closest genres to family history writing) do have to deal with the problem of how to write about the unknowable, it is a recurring problem within any family history. We encounter the problem of repetition in every generation as we say that yet another person was born, married and died, did the same type of job or lived in the same area. There are also limited resources to construct a story from.

This guide focuses on ways to overcome these problems. It explores how to structure a piece of work, develop your writing skills, add social and historical context to make it interesting and steps you can take to wean yourself off researching and start writing. Throughout are a range of practical tips and exercises which encourage you to see your work through the eyes of the reader in order to develop a readable ancestral story. Included is guidance on the various formats a family history can take, including methods of production and publishing.

Many of the writing exercises are adapted from those used by writers of fiction. Nevertheless, I tend to lean towards those that have a close relationship to family history; in particular, biography, histories and historical fiction. It is not necessary to try every exercise or adopt every piece of advice in this guide. These are tools to be used where needed. Nevertheless, writing is a skill that can be developed and it can be beneficial to try new and different approaches. These may provide you with a fresh perspective, a chance to tighten up what you have already written, make it more interesting or simply confirm that what you have done is fine.

Chapter 1 looks at how to start writing, choosing a format and writing style, what to include (or not), making a plan, setting goals and deadlines and what to do if your research is not finished. As well as focusing on the planning and organisational stages this chapter considers the questions of who you are writing for and whose history it is.

There is a separate chapter on developing writing skills. This focuses on bringing life to the page. Included are suggestions on how to get constructive feedback from others and find writing support. There is obviously some crossover between developing writing skills and the next chapter on 'make it interesting'. The problems of repetition, missing pieces, gaps and contradictions begin to be addressed here. Of particular importance is how to find and use authentic local and social history sources to add context.

Although the format of this book takes a sequential approach – starting out, adding historical context and ending with publishing – there is an argument for planning your layout before you begin or soon afterwards. The Nitty-Gritty chapter deals with all the practical issues not covered elsewhere such as lists of sources; confidentiality; when and how to use other people's work and issues of copyright; reproducing images; citations and quotes.

The last chapter looks at publishing, from print versions and e-Books to blogs and websites. This includes practical tips on design, layout, integrating illustrations and printing and binding. At the end of this book is a Directory of Useful Resources which lists all the addresses and websites mentioned throughout plus others of general use and a Select Bibliography.

Finally, I would make a plea that you share your family history with others. As well as family members, give copies to your local family history society and the Society of Genealogists in London. You don't have to be a member to do this. Who knows who might pick up a copy in the future and find a connection to your ancestry?

Chapter 1

WHAT KIND OF ANCESTRAL STORY

Your family history can be anything from a book detailing every known ancestor or series of mini biographies and newsletters to a website or blog. However, it is crucial to start with some idea of how to frame your ancestral story in order to make decisions on what to include, and how. Even in non-fiction you are telling a story. By creating a strong framework for your characters and key events it is possible to create an interesting and entertaining tale that compels the reader to continue reading.

A typical family history book might look something like this. Websites and blogs would have separate pages or links instead of chapters:

- Title page.
- Contents page.
- Preface.
- Acknowledgements.
- Foreword/Introduction.
- Timeline.
- Family Tree(s).
- Chapters 1 to 5: The Marris family line.
- Chapters 6 to 10: The Ismay family line.
- Other chapters on specific places, occupations or events (these might go in between some of the family chapters above).
- Final chapter – bringing it all together.
- Appendices. This could be research notes, an overview of findings, family trees, a glossary, additional information on people and places, etc.
- Endnotes and footnotes (if you choose to use them). These can go at either the end of each chapter or as a separate list at the back of the book.
- Indexes to family names, subjects and places (if you choose to).
- List of sources and bibliography.

Ask most people what they think a written family history will look like and they will say 'a book'. There is something about a book which lends

Here and overleaf: Some examples of different family histories produced for clients in a variety of bindings from card to full leather.

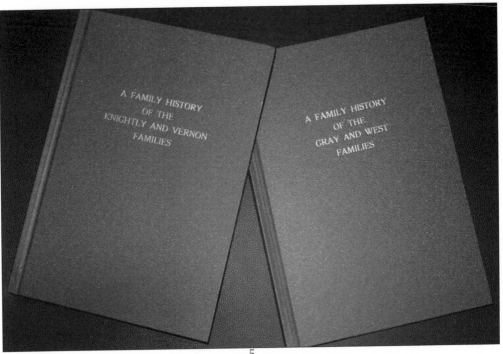

Postcard of Rustic Cottage in Stansted, 1910

Essex malt was widely sold to local breweries, private customers and, from the 1750s onwards, to London using local rivers for transport. In *'Essex at Work, 1700-1815'* the author uses quarters as a means of measuring how much malt was sold, and describes Stansted Mountfitchet as producing 3,663 quarters in 1754 alone.

Stansted Mountfitchet castle is the only Norman motte and bailey castle in the world. It was originally an Iron Age fort then later a Saxon and Viking village. When the Normans came, their most important centre in this area of Essex was Stansted, where Robert Gernon, one of the greatest landowners under William the Conqueror, established his headquarters at Stansted Castle. His estate was passed on to the Mountfitchets, who gave their name to the village.

The Mountfitcher's were amongst those who led the opposition to King John, and owned land at Runnymede, where Magna Carta was signed, which is why the words Magna Carta and the effigy of a knight appear on the village sign.

Stansted Village Signpost, 2008

During the barons' wars with King John the castle was destroyed and Stansted gradually lost its significance. The modern replica of the castle is now a tourist attraction and its church of St. Mary, still has many Norman features.

This area of Essex has a strong Nonconformist tradition, going back to John Bapley, vicar of nearby Manuden, who was burnt at the stake in 1430 as a follower of Wycliffe. The area around Stansted has always had strong sporting traditions, with the cricket ground at Rickling well known nationally as well as being the home of many families and individuals who have made their mark in the country as a whole, such as The Gilbeys, wine merchants who lived at Elsenham Hall for a while.

An old Roman road known as 'Stanestreet' runs between Colchester and St. Albans. This was so well used that in 1530 the canons of Thremhall Priory, just

itself to telling the story of several generations of people. However, breaking down a family history into smaller stand alone projects makes writing it more achievable and probably more interesting in the long run.

The ideal format for many people is a series of mini biographies or booklets which focus on either one generation or individual at a time or a particular place, event, theme or occupation. These can then be built up into something bigger over time. This approach can be used equally well for those who want to produce newsletters, blogs and websites. This is not meant to deter anyone from attempting to write a book, but is simply advice about setting achievable goals because of the amount of work and time it can take to write a book.

The average novel is between 50,000 and 80,000 words. It can take months, sometimes years, of full-time work to write something of this length. I have written a large number of family histories about my own ancestors and for clients. The average length is around quarter to half of these figures, depending on the number of generations and amount of background detail.

One book I recently produced included two family lines (the ancestors of four grandparents) from the early 1800s to the present day. The total number of words is 22,660 on 160 sides of A4, not including the list of sources and bibliography. There are seven chapters, a foreword and timeline. The timeline is 1,967 words. The shortest chapter is 842 words and the longest 5,996. Every chapter includes copies of documents, photographs and other images, plus some local and social history.

Tips

- You can get a rough estimate of total length by multiplying the average length of chapters given above by the number of generations to be included. One of my lines has six generations coming forwards from 1801 to my parents, whilst another has eight from the early 1700s.
- Using a rough average of between 2,000 and 5,000 words for each chapter or section, the total length will be between 12,000 and 30,000 for a 6-generation family and 16,000 and 40,000 for an 8-generation family.
- For shorter projects such as booklets, websites and blogs a useful rough guide is between 500 and 2,000 words for each section.

Another great advantage of this approach is that you do not have to produce a chronological account or even focus on just one line. Instead you can treat each mini biography as a story in its own right or gradually link them to others. Such smaller projects should never be seen as a compromise or less crafted. One of the first pieces I ever wrote was about my maternal grandmother and her immediate family. This later became a chapter within a bigger book. In short, be ambitious, but be realistic.

Which Ancestors?

One of the hardest decisions is which ancestors and family lines to include in a written history. One of the most common approaches is a 'single line of descent' history. This begins with the earliest known ancestor for a particular surname (male or female). It then brings their story forwards down the generations to whatever point you choose to stop. Each chapter or section focuses on the direct ancestor in that line.

Taking my own Camplejohn ancestors as an example I would start with the earliest known, a Miles Camplejohn who married in 1707 and died in 1722. The first chapter would focus on him, his wife and four children. The next chapter would focus on his son Robert Camplejohn (1711–1766) who was the next in this direct line. Again, his biography would incorporate information on his wife and all his children. The next chapter would move on to Robert's son William (1747–1800), then on again to William's son Anthony (1784–1803) and so on.

Family photograph of the Naughtons outside their home, 1950s.

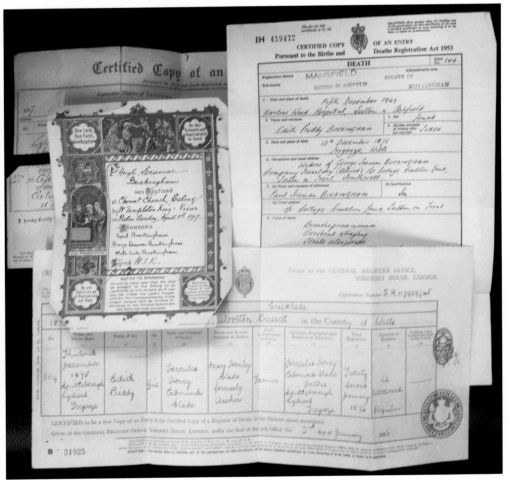

Family memorabilia – birth and baptismal certificates.

Because each person in the direct line has their own separate biography I only introduce them briefly in the parent's story. For example: 'Anthony Camplejohn was born in 1784, sixth child out of seven born to William and Ann Camplejohn (née Emitt)'. Or, 'William and Ann Camplejohn (née Emitt) had seven children: Robert, 1774; William, 1776; John, 1778; Richard, 1779; Ann, 1781–1793; Anthony, 1784; and another Ann, 1798–1803'. I would then follow with a line that said something along the lines of how Anthony's story features in a later chapter. I then carry on the story of his parents and siblings in this one.

There are no rules about the amount of detail that should be included about every family member. However, most do not go into any depth on siblings. Rather, they just provide the dates of birth or baptism, death or burial of siblings unless they did something significant. Some do go a little further and list the marriages and children. An expanded version of this is the 'all-in-one' family tree, which includes everything that is known about every family member, but still arranging it around the direct ancestor in each line.

You may decide to write a history about more than one family line so that two or four (or more) distinct families are joined together. Typically, this would either be arranged into separate sections within a book, or as separate books. For my Blanchard and Panting grandparents the history is split into three parts. Part one is the Blanchard line. Part two starts after I get to my grandfather's generation and his marriage into the Panting family and focuses on the Panting line. Part three starts where the two families join and brings it forwards to the present day. If I were to split the two lines into separate books then one would probably end with the marriage of this couple, whilst the other would take it forward to the present day.

Tip
- A good method to begin with is to write a short summary about one family grouping in your family line as in my Camplejohn example. Splitting up each generation into small pieces enables you to start the process of making each person stand out from other family members and who should have their own chapter or section.

Exercise
- Choose three or four people on your family tree.
- Write a couple of simple sentences describing when and where they were born or baptised, married and died or buried as in this example: 'Miles Camplejohn was born some time in the late 1600s. He married Mary Abbot in Riccall in Yorkshire in 1707 and died in the same parish in 1722'.
- Now list their children and move on to the next in line. For example, 'Miles and Mary Camplejohn had four children called John, Robert, Elizabeth and Miles baptised in Riccall between 1708 and February 1720/21. The next in this family line was their son Robert who was baptised in 1711. He married Elizabeth Wright in Riccall in 1735 and they had had nine Camplejohn children baptised between 1736 and 1756'.
- Repeat the process until every person on your tree has a sentence written about them.

The expanded 'all-in-one' family history is very appealing to family historians as we do not, in general, like omitting even the smallest details about our ancestors. The main problems are manageability and tedium for the reader. Going back to Miles and Mary Camplejohn again, one method I use is to divide their chapter into clearly defined sections using sub-headings so that each child of those parents effectively gets their own biography.

There is a danger with this approach of confusing the reader with lots of repetition and going backwards and forwards. As one generation can cover a large time period it is entirely possible to have parents still having children when their grandchildren begin to be born. As a result it can be hard to keep track of people. Moreover, placing people from different generations into a social and historical context becomes tricky if they lived through many of the same events and had similar experiences.

The main issue is to make sure the reader does not lose track of who is who. So for example, Miles and Mary's son Richard (1750/51–1764) would have his own section. Once I finished his story I would start a new section for the next sibling, making sure it was clearly headed. I make sure to remind the reader throughout how each of these people fits in with Mary and Miles and that we are still talking about one generation. At the end of writing about each of their children, I then go back to the parents to finish off their story – often the end of the parents' lives. This device allows me to create a direct link to the next generation by ending their chapter with a sentence about who comes next.

If there are a lot of children or information for some of the siblings then I might create separate chapters for each one. This requires clearly defined links to the parents and next direct generation (in this case Robert). Otherwise, a reader may not be able to work out who it is that comes next in the ancestral line.

These problems can be overcome with careful structuring, the use of sub-titles and the inclusion of mini family trees or timelines. A useful technique is to remind your reader of who people were and how they relate to each other by using phrases like 'Miles's second son . . .'; 'George Marris went into the same line of work as his uncle Barker Marris', or, 'Barker's nephew George followed in his footsteps as a . . .'.

Putting it Together

Having decided on the overall format and who to include, the next stage is to break it down further into a clear and readable structure of chapters, pages (for websites and blogs) or sections. Books, booklets or mini biographies need separate chapters with text further divided into sections or sub-headings for particular individuals or generations, events and so on. With blogs and websites the decision is whether to have separate pages or to use techniques such as highlighted links to stand alone sections on one large page.

Beginnings and endings frame everything that comes in between, so consider early on how to start and finish your tale. There is no right or wrong way to start and end. Many family histories simply start with the earliest known ancestor then move forwards chronologically. Others use a significant event, a place or piece of family memorabilia, the death of a relative or family gathering as a means of reflecting on what has gone before or since. One of my distant cousins used the object approach when writing a piece which began with her mother's button box and the memories it evoked.

How you finish off is just as important as the beginning. This applies to each ancestor or line as much as the whole project. You might wrap up with a family gathering, a wedding, birth or death. A copy of a funeral eulogy is an eloquent and moving reminder of the passage of time. Alternatively, you could provide a short review of the whole ancestral tale that highlights key turning points or memorable events. Quotations, poems or lines from songs are popular as a full stop, whilst some family historians prefer to end with the possibility of more to come by reflecting on what has still to be found out or lines yet to be researched.

Layout

How a piece of work is put together physically is another important element in what makes it readable. It doesn't matter how much interesting material you have, if it is crammed in amongst lots of genealogical detail without thought then it can confuse the reader. If, for example, there is a long piece about someone's occupation just stuck into the middle of other text then it can be clumsy and distracting.

Leaving aside the question of what type of context to include for now (see Chapter 4, 'Make it Interesting'), what needs to be considered is how and where to put it. This is where decisions need to be made about whether long pieces of text should be separated out, given sub-headings or put into information boxes or sidebars. People's attentions spans can be very short, particularly if reading something they do not know much about. When we describe a piece of writing as 'engaging' it is because it is relevant and has been delivered in an interesting manner regardless of what we already know on the subject.

Tips
- There are no rules on how to blend social, historical and geographical material. Try going through a selection of family histories, general histories, biographies and memoirs and noting where and how other authors include such material and which methods appeal to you. As

you do, see how much detail is included and how details are linked together.

- Apply this analysis to your own work by briefly noting ideas on how such techniques can be used to link pivotal events such as births, marriages and deaths, illness or migration with particular aspects of local and social history.
- Assess each piece of information for relevance by asking why it is there and what it adds to the narrative. If it does not fit in remove it regardless of how beautifully written or clever it is.

Contents Page, Preface and Foreword or Introduction

A contents page creates a professional look as well as letting readers know what is included. This is a draft for the history of my Panting ancestors.

Introduction
Timeline   pages i–xx
Chapter One   The Gloucestershire Years   pages 1–50
Chapter Two   The Move to County Durham   pages 51–60
Chapter Three   Charles Smith Panting   pages 61–70
Chapter Four   Dorothy May (Maisie) Panting   pages 71–80
Chapter Five   The Panting and Blanchard
                 Families Merge   pages 81–90
Appendices   i) Outline of Research   pages 91–100
                 ii) Transcripts and Documents   pages101–150
Family Trees
Sources and Bibliography
Index

The preface is traditionally where the writer speaks personally about how and why they have produced this work. This is a good place to mention any personal interests which are reflected in it and acknowledge those who have helped you in any way. Don't forget to put the date it was completed.

The introduction sets the scene, often briefly summarising the contents of each chapter or section. Many authors combine it with a preface to explain how and why their project came into being. This means that whilst it is usually the first part of a book that we read the introduction is usually the last to be finished. If not, it will almost certainly need rewriting or restrict how your project develops. Any particular obstacles, gaps or exciting discoveries can be mentioned in a general outline of the research you have done. For example:

The history of this family was uncovered through a range of sources including census returns, parish registers and wills. One major brick wall was broken down through investigating the manorial records, whilst the tithe and enclosure maps provided a wonderful visual image of where they lived in the early 1800s.

For one of my own family histories I began with an explanation of what had been done, what I had found and any gaps that still needed filling. I used part of the introduction to draw attention to the recollections of my great aunt Eleanor Blanchard as these provided invaluable insights into the personalities of some of my ancestors.

More generally, the introduction allows space to discuss problems of lack of evidence, your own theories and if you have engaged in fictionalising in order to fill in gaps. You might mention areas that are still to be investigated. This enables your reader to see what inspired you to produce a family history and any particular influences that have shaped what you have done.

Chapters and Sections, Mini Biographies and Interludes

In general, the most practical approach is to divide a family history into distinct chapters or sections for every generation or key figure. Effectively, each of these is a mini biography. For example, when I wrote about my ancestor Elizabeth Bell Marris I wrote one chapter on her parents Barker and Margaret Marris. Within this is a separate section sub-titled: 'The children of Barker and Margaret Marris'. This sub-section has separate details of each of these children. Because Elizabeth Bell Marris is the direct line being followed I only mention her briefly in the chapter on her parents as follows:

> Barker and Margaret Marris had twelve children born between 1856 and 1875 in Scotter and Scotton in Lincolnshire. Their eldest, Georgeana Mary, was baptised in Scotter less than eight months after her parent's marriage.
>
> The eighth child, Elizabeth Bell Marris (known as Belle), was born in April 1868 and named after an elder sister Elizabeth, who had died at the age of 2 just two years earlier. Belle is the next direct descendant in this family line and her story continues in full in the next chapter.

After writing about the children in one generation I tend to fill in other details about the parents' lives not already covered such as Barker and Margaret Marris moving to Yorkshire in the 1870s. I tend to finish with each generational chapter with the deaths of the key characters or a summary of what is known about the rest of their children and those children's descendants. For example, 'by the time Barker and Margaret both died in 1903 their surviving children were all married and having children themselves'. I can then lead directly into the next chapter by using a variation of the line above about who comes next.

Where a family member did something particularly interesting or was involved in a major historical event which results in a particular section becoming very large then I usually separate out those details. This can be done in the form of an interlude without disrupting the main text. Where there are short pieces of additional information then these can fit well into a text box, especially if they accompany an image. These can be given a different background colour so as to stand out. One such example was when I placed a text box next to a copy of a baptism in order to emphasise a point in the text about a possible error in a parish register.

An interlude allows the author to digress into relevant topics in a separate short chapter; in other words an interval. This is used to very good effect in the biography of Mrs Beeton by Kathryn Hughes to explore topics such as food adulteration, historical changes in housekeeping and cooking and women's legal and political status in the nineteenth century (*The Short Life & Long Times of Mrs Beeton*, Fourth Estate, 2005). Maureen Waller also uses this technique in her history of marriage (*The English Marriage*, John Murray, 2010) to introduce case studies and examples.

Calling these diversions an 'interlude' or just giving them a clear title of their own makes it very clear that they stand slightly apart from the main story. In my own writing I make sure I have a strong link sentence to bring the reader back to the main story at the end of the digression. I find it helpful to remind the reader why such a digression was needed. For instance, by directly referring back to a move, birth, marriage, death or job opportunity. This keeps the chronology intact so as not to confuse the reader. The following is an extract of an interlude about witch trials and persecution in Essex. This appears in a family's history because one of their tenants was prosecuted for taking part in a 'ducking which resulted in a woman's death'. A page from another section of the same interlude can be seen in the accompanying illustration.

Essex was at the heart of the infamous witch trials which dominated England in the seventeenth century. Trials, duckings, persecutions and executions occurred across the county, with several cases in villages close to Colchester, and at least two cases recorded in Alresford itself.

According to the historians Cohn and Kieckhefer, writing in the 1970s, the origins of the witch hunts that swept across Europe in the

By this time the English Civil War was underway, and Hopkins and Stearne were able to travel England claiming to be sanctioned by Parliament, though the office of Witchfinder General was never officially recognised. Parliament in fact expressed concern about Hopkins' methods of obtaining confessions and began an enquiry, but before that could be completed Hopkins had retired. He died in 1647, at his home in Essex. Legend says that he was executed as a witch, but his burial is recorded in the parish register for the church of St Mary at Mistley, which would not be the case if he had been condemned as a witch.

A section of an interlude on witch hunting in Essex.

Frontispiece from 'The Discovery of Witches', 1647, by Matthew Hopkins

Middle Ages can be traced back to Switzerland and Croatia. Concerned by what they thought were instances of witchcraft the people pressed the civil courts to support them, and the movement spread. Whilst Pope John XXII had granted the powers to the Inquisition in 1320 to allow them to search out and prosecute sorcerers, the inquisitorial courts became involved in systemic witch hunts only in the fifteenth century . . .

Another interlude in a separate book focused on the shoe-making industry in Norfolk. The extract below was accompanied by images of shoe-making equipment from that period and drawings and paintings of shoe-makers at work:

Shoemaking thrived in Norfolk until the mid twentieth century, when, like so many other manufacturing industries it suffered from overseas competition. Until relatively recently, every village in Norfolk would have had a shoemaker. Norwich had been a centre of this trade since the early eighteenth century and became the home of international companies such Clarke's and Start-rite, who amongst other work, produced boots for the British army and its allies during the First World War.

Traditionally, boots were bought by labourers each year in preparation for the coming winter with the extra money they earned at harvest time. The wealthy might buy fashionable shoes from London makers, but skilled local crasftmen could copy and produce their own versions. Local manufacturers such as William would have benefitted from the growing success and reputation of firms in the city.

By the 1860s the numbers of people working in the shoe trade had expanded enormously whilst other traditional industries such as the textiles trade were in decline. In the mid nineteenth century some shoemaking processes were undertaken in factories, but the majority of work was still carried out as outwork either as individual shoemakers or garret masters who employed a few people in small workshops. By 1900 the processes involved had become fully mechanised and the small independent shoemakers and leather cutters began to die out, although some adapted by specialising in shoe repairs . . .

Within each chapter I tend to use sub-headings with titles in different font sizes so that it is clear how a particular child or event fits in with the key figures that chapter is devoted to. Other sub-sections would include social and historical context. So a typical chapter would be structured something like this:

Chapter Heading: George and Mary Ismay (née Bell)
The main biographical details of this couple would be entered here.

Sub-heading or interlude: Whickham, County Durham
Background history on a place usually gets it own sub-section.

Sub-heading: The children of George and Mary Ismay
Within this sub-section would be mini biographies of each of this couple's six children. Each of these would have their own sub-title in a smaller font. For example: *Samuel Ismay, 1830–1908*.

You may find, as I often do, that once you start writing you begin to change the format. This is usually as a result of having large amounts of detail. With a large family, or one where I know a lot about cousins, children and grandchildren more distantly removed from the main lines, then it is sometimes necessary to create completely separate chapters for every child within a generation. This is where having strong linking sentences and reminders of who people are and how they relate will help the reader keep track.

Tip

- Readers can get easily confused by lots of genealogical detail. Keep reminding them where they are and how people connect. For instance, when writing about the twelve children of Barker and Margaret Marris I would remind the reader that I am still talking about their children each time I move on from one to another. For example: 'Margaret Hannah Marris, the youngest child of Barker and Margaret, was born in 1875, almost twenty years after their first child'.

Exercise

- Practise structuring a piece of text without losing the strand of the story by writing a short piece about one couple and their children in a similar format to the examples given here.

Themes

Many family histories suit being organised into themes focused on a place, event or occupation such as 'The Wheelwright Blanchards'. Many of the families I have written about have been farmers or agricultural labourers. In such cases I tend to create one in-depth piece about the history of farming and agriculture in their area. Where significant changes occurred that relate to a particular person or generation I bring that in to their chapter, as in this extract:

> By the time William married in 1917 he had moved from Suffolk to Lancashire. The north of England offered many opportunities to farm workers in this period whose lives were characterized by hard work, low pay and poverty. Farming had been in decline since the 1880s due to a mixture of cheap imports from other countries, several years of bad weather and poor harvests. These factors exacerbated a population movement away from rural areas that had begun in the early 1800s.

Themes work extremely well where an ancestor had a particularly eventful life or you have wide range of information and documents relating to them. A book recently published on a medieval Norfolk merchant called Robert Toppes is a very good example of this format. It includes separate chapters on his house, his will, the trade guild to which he belonged and the city he lived in (Richard Matthews, *Robert Toppes Medieval Mercer of Norwich*, Norfolk and Norwich Heritage Trust, 2013).

Timelines

Timelines are a wonderful multi-purpose genealogical tool, and one of the best methods I know for creating a framework on which to hang a narrative. They allow you to add context to your family history as can be seen in Chapter 4, 'Make it Interesting', as well as being an excellent means for spotting gaps and anomalies.

Tip

- Create a timeline for each ancestor as a means of organising your research before starting writing. Note any gaps in knowledge and aspects that need following up. This will enable you to decide whether or not you need to do any additional research. A timeline I drew for my ancestor John Charles Panting looked something like this:

Facts and Sources	Not Known	Action Needed
Born in Fairford, Gloucestershire, circa 1825	Parents' names Baptism	Marriage certificate ordered Search Fairford parish registers
Listed by only his middle name Charles on most records	Any siblings? When died? – after 1891	Re-check BMD indexes and earlier census returns
Moved to County Durham before 1866	Full details of all children	
Married Phyllis Smith 1866 (born circa 1837)	Details of wife's Smith family	Local history – museums and archives
Nine children born in County Durham	Where he worked	Working life
Brother-in-law Joseph Smith living with them 1881	Religion – grandchildren Baptists	
Mining engineer		
Sources: census returns, BMDs, family stories, Consett parish registers		

A variation on this format can be seen in the timeline I created for my ancestor Barker Marris. In my mini timeline I noted the dates, information known from birth, marriage and death certificates, photographs, census returns, parish registers and so on. I then added a list of what I would like to find out. In a separate notes column I included brief details of family tales and rumours. Here I also added comments about any matters affecting the research process such as illegible or destroyed records. Once finished, I took the timeline outline and wrote the details up into short paragraphs. I occasionally add a column for action that needs to be taken.

Date	Information	Not Known	Notes
1826	Baptised Scotter, Lincolnshire to William and Sarah Brother Charles born circa 1842 listed on census	How many siblings? Mother's maiden name?	Church and village visited – photographs Action – find out what happened to siblings
1841	Living in Scotter and working as a servant	What did he do as a servant?	Copy of census Action – find out about local history
1841–1851	Moves to Barnetby Le Wold	How did he move?	Action – find out what forms of travel there were and likely routes
1851	Living in Barnetby Le Wold and working as a servant	When and why did he move here?	Copy of census and trade directories
1851–1856	Moves to Scotton	When did he move here?	
1856 7 February	Marries Hannah Margaret Ismay in Scotton church		Copy of marriage entry Photographs of them when old

Exercise

- Create your own timeline of facts, missing pieces and action needed for an ancestor.
- Include a list of documents and photographs you have for them.
- Now write up the first two or three facts from the timeline into a couple of short paragraphs. For example, 'John Charles Panting was always known by his middle name. By the time he married in 1866 he had moved from Gloucestershire to County Durham where he worked as a mining engineer'.
- Look at what you have written and note where you might want to insert these copies of documents or photographs.

Family Trees

Drawing up a family tree provides a useful framework to keep your research on track. Mini family trees are an excellent way to show the reader how everything fits together. It can be helpful to work through each branch chronologically if you are stuck with writing and just write a sentence or

Knightly Timeline

1760-1820	**George III**
1787	First fleet of convicts sails to Australia
c.1792	**Birth of Samuel Silvester Knightly in Aldgate, London**
c.1793	**Birth of Charlotte Ward in Marylebone**
1798	Society of United Irishmen rebel against British rule in Ireland
1801	Act of Union unites Britain and Ireland
	First National census taken
1803	Britain declares war on France
1805	Battle of Trafalgar
1809	Prison reformer Elizabeth Fry moves to Plashet House in East Ham
1811-1812	Luddite riots
1815	Battle of Waterloo: Napoleon defeated
	National agricultural depression
1816	**Marriage of Samuel Silvester Knightly and Charlotte Ward at St. George Hanover Square church**
1817-1823	**4 children born to Samuel Silvester and Charlotte Knightly in Shoreditch**
1818	Mary Shelley's *Frankenstein* published
1819	Peterloo Massacre
1820-1830	**George IV**
1820	Regents Canal opens
1821	**Birth of Samuel Knightly to Samuel Silvester and Charlotte**
1823	Sir Robert Peel reforms the criminal law and penal system
1825	First passenger steam railroad from Stockton-on-Tees to Darlington
c.1826	**Birth of Mary Elizabeth Riley in Penshurst**
1829-1847	Catholic Emancipation Act
1830-1837	**William IV**
1832	Parliamentary Reform Act
	Cholera epidemic in Europe: 31,000 people killed in Britain
1833	Factory Act restricts working hours for women and children
1834	Municipal Reform Act
	'Tolpuddle Martyrs' transported
	Slave trade abolished in British empire
1837-1901	**Queen Victoria**
1838-1848	Chartist movement
1840	Penny post and vaccination for the poor introduced
	Shoreditch railway station opens

Example of a timeline.

National and Local Events	Date	The Abbott Family
Tithe Commutation Act overhauls the system of giving tithes to support the church and clergy	1836	
Queen Victoria	1837-1901	
Smallpox epidemic	1837-1840	
Tithe Maps for Needham Market and Mickfield drawn up	1837	
Chartist movement	1838-1848	
Penny post introduced. Vaccination against smallpox implemented within workhouses	1840	
	c 1841 - 1846	Charles Abbott resident in Barham Workhouse
National Census taken. First to include people's names. Thomas Cook arranges his first excursion	1841	Charles Abbott listed in Barham Workhouse on the census Robert Abbott resident in Mickfield
Chartist riots Lord Shaftesbury's Mines Act Death of agricultural reformer 'Coke of Norfolk'	1842	Death of Elizabeth Abbott (née Wingfield)
Death of prison reformer Elizabeth Fry and anti-slavery campaigner Sir Thomas Buxton	1845	
Repeal of Corn Laws	1846	Death of Charles Abbott in Barham Workhouse

Another example of a timeline.

paragraph about each person. The genealogy reports generated by some family tree programmes can be used in a similar manner and worked up into something more comprehensive.

Appendices, Indexes, Footnotes, Endnotes and Sources

Appendices are a storage place for information that does not fit easily into the main body of writing. Typically, they might include transcripts of documents; copies of research reports; a description of how the research was conducted; theories or explanations of terminology or obscure and old trades and occupations.

Name and subject indexes enable the reader to find particular people or items of interest. A place index is useful if your ancestors moved around a lot. Source citations are an essential part of any book concerned with presenting research findings. They provide credibility to your research and leave a trail others can follow.

Approach, Style and Tone

As family histories are biographical and factual accounts the majority are written in the third person with the author acting as an observational narrator talking to the audience. This direct voice works very well in drawing attention to the passage of time and key events. Such an approach allows room for the narrator to step in and add explanations, pose theories and questions and highlight where there are gaps in knowledge.

Writing in the first person – using 'I' throughout – is less common unless you include memoir or an account of the research process. A humorous account along these lines is *My Family and other Animals: Adventures in Genealogy* by Jeremy Hardy (Ebury Press, 2010). In it, the author describes his discoveries and the people he met along the way.

There tends to be no or very little dialogue. This can put the family historian at a disadvantage compared to fiction writers as dialogue directly conveys information and introduces thoughts and feelings. In contrast, dialogue in non-fiction tends to appear stilted and contrived unless the author is a very skilled writer. Any such awkwardness runs the risk of making your work seem unbelievable. Dialogue is however used more extensively, and to great effect, in fictionalised family histories.

In a family history, speech tends to be recreated through quoting from memoirs, oral histories, diaries, letters, songs and newspaper reports. The difference is that such sources are by their nature rather one-sided so there is rarely the sense of witnessing a conversation that occurs in fiction. Whilst these are people's own words, they are not presented in quite the same way as they would be in fiction.

Attitudes and Viewpoints

Whilst it is important to say things in your own way it is essential that this does not alienate or patronise those who want to read it. To present any written history in a credible manner it is essential to avoid making sweeping statements, unsubstantiated generalisations, presenting an inflexible or narrow perspective or misinterpreting the past.

More specifically, do not assume that other people share the same world view as you. As soon as we start to explain events and people's actions then we are formulating theories, and it is quite possible for there to be more than one explanation or theory of the same event. Perhaps even more important is to avoid placing a modern viewpoint onto our ancestors or judging their actions with the benefit of hindsight.

You may make discoveries that completely change your timeline of events, what you believe about a particular ancestor, or that an ancestor behaved in an abhorrent manner. Any good genealogist will explore all evidence they come across thoroughly, even if what is uncovered turns out to be shocking or the complete opposite of family beliefs. Of course there may be mitigating circumstances or evidence of a miscarriage of justice, but it is important not to be carried away with the strength of your own convictions and ignore evidence to the contrary. If you do, your readers will not believe other statements you make.

Tip

- Survey a range of history, memoir, biographical and genealogy books and look at how they are structured, the writing style and what kept you reading, what you like and don't like and why. Include privately published family histories held at family history societies, record offices and libraries. Ask other people their opinions on the same choices.

'I' or 'They'

Think about whether you are going to put yourself into the book and if so, how 'present' you might be. In this book 'I' am very much present, commenting on how I have gone about writing and providing examples from my own experience. This approach allows you as the narrator to comment directly on aspects such an unknown facts, theories and controversies. A good example of a fascinating piece of social history where the author uses this approach is *The Lodger: Shakespeare on Silver Street* by Charles Nicholl (Penguin, 2007) in which he is quietly present via his commentary on sources in relation to Shakespeare's life and work.

Other narrators remove themselves even further into the background keeping their language as neutral and non-personal as possible. This tends to be the approach found in traditional histories and biographies. Most family histories contain a mix, with the narrator staying out of the limelight, almost voice-over style, only stepping in where an explanation or interpretation is needed. Again, exceptions to this occur, especially in histories that actively incorporate the research process or the narrator's personal journey of discovery as part of the story.

Present or Past Tense

There is no rule to say you must write about the past in the past tense, or stick to only one or the other. Nevertheless, without care, mixing tenses can cause problems with consistency, whilst writing about the past in the present tense can read very oddly. For instance, a typical account of where people were living when various census returns were taken might read: 'In 1851, John and Mary were living at 41 Chesterfield Road. By the time the 1861 census was taken they had moved to . . .'. Now see what happens with that second sentence when written in the present tense: 'In 1851, John and Mary live at number 41 Chesterfield Road. By 1861 they live at . . .'. The key is to make sure it is clear and that the text flows smoothly throughout.

Tip
- If you are unsure which tense a piece of writing should be in then write it out in both forms. Then read it aloud to hear how the text flows and whether there are any jarring notes.

Fictionalised Family Histories
Some of the most interesting and entertaining family histories I have read were fictionalised accounts. Fictionalising a family history can get round some of the problems of how to build tension and pace, develop characters and omit boring and repetitive information by using novelistic techniques. A good example is Kate Atkinson's *Behind the Scenes at the Museum* (Black Swan, 1998). Many historical novels use this format successfully by blending facts and quotes from diaries, letters and memoirs with imagined thoughts and feelings that could not be known by the author. There is however an obligation on you to make it absolutely clear which elements are fiction. This can be done in an introduction or in the text by the use of phrases such as 'I picture', 'I like to imagine,' 'I can imagine' or 'one wonders if'.

Co-authoring
Writing with other people can add a whole new dimension to a family history. Unless you keep your contributions as completely separate pieces it allows a wider range of perspectives, voice and style. If you do co-author then it is important to set some ground rules about who will do what, who is going to proofread, who has editorial control and how to give feedback. You might of course simply write your own pieces and join them together. This has the benefit of avoiding potential tensions over differing styles and approach.

Who For and Whose Story?
It is essential to think about who is going to read your work and what your aims are. People who write factual books are often asked if they want to

inform, educate or entertain as this affects the approach taken. I would argue that the best and most effective way to 'inform' is to entertain your reader. At the same time you will find you are 'educating', although the reader may be unaware of it. Deciding what your aims are and who it is aimed at will influence the shape, tone, format and style of your writing.

A related question on style is whether to take a chatty and familiar tone or something more formal. Writing for different people requires different styles. The scholarly approach tends to use conventional academic format, including detailed source references, footnotes or endnotes and appendices. The latter often appears more authoritative (whether it really is or not), but the friendly approach can hold people's attention better. The most appealing family histories tend to be written in a non-academic storytelling style, with no, or minimal, footnotes or endnotes.

References to sources are generally integrated into the text so as not to lose the narrative flow, although I would stress how important it is to still provide a full list of all sources used in a separate appendix along with a select bibliography. If you have ever found yourself wondering 'how do they know that' when you read something then you will appreciate the importance of providing a list of what you searched. If you do not then a reader could well wonder how reliable or rigorous it really is.

When we write about real people we need to ask whose story is it. All authors tell their own version of events. As such, you will not please everyone. Whilst any aspects open to interpretation should be acknowledged in order to retain your integrity as a family history biographer, it is your story. Unless you have passed false information off as truth then you have nothing to apologise for. Even more important is to not worry about whether others agree with your interpretations or how you have presented it. If you have been rigorous in your research, made it clear when you don't know something and used authentic secondary sources to build your background then you can be confident that you have produced something that will stand the test of time.

What and How Much to Include

The question of what to include and what to leave out is a huge dilemma for genealogists as a good researcher will always want to know the source and see proof. Most histories do not provide the reader with every detail uncovered or show every document found. These minutiae can be added to an appendix or put onto a website, CD or memory stick to share.

Only you can decide how much detail to go into, but unless you know your readers tastes extremely well then I recommend a light touch. Do not worry that you might be telling your reader something they already know.

Most people will be more than happy to have their knowledge reinforced (we all like to feel clever). This does of course come back to the question of where to find reliable sources of information on those aspects we don't know. You probably don't need to explain much if what you are writing about is obvious or straightforward.

You may not know much more than where they were baptised, married and buried (and maybe not all of those!). I look more closely at how to fill in those gaps in another section in this book. Nevertheless, it is worth considering when deciding on your style and approach. If you are going to add a lot of background detail your style will be influenced by whether it includes lots of quotes or paraphrasing and the type of sources used.

One of the biggest problems in writing a family history is how to integrate a huge mass of material. You need to demonstrate your knowledge without being too technical. You do not have to include everything. Many written family histories are little more than a boring list of names and dates or simply pack in so much it is overwhelming to the reader, who then gives up. One biography I recently read suffered from this problem. As a professional genealogist I can keep mental track of names and relationships very well, but still found myself flicking backwards and forwards in order to make sense of it. In the end I gave up.

With my Ismay line I gave a brief outline in my introduction of the key sources used to trace them. In the main story I wanted to flag up some of the obstacles that held up research and how they were overcome as this process of discovery is as important to the story. Nevertheless, I am well aware that even the keenest genealogist may not wish to read about every step I took. Instead I simply brought in the occasional mention where it fitted with the story. For instance, discovering when the family moved from Northumberland to Kent and questions I had such as how people met. A separate, more detailed account of the steps taken and discoveries made could then be put into an appendix for those who want to read it.

Tip

- Always question what is relevant to the story. Make sure it is not an unnecessary diversion just because it is of interest to you.

One of my writing projects has the themes of 'New Country, New Life', 'Mine Workers' and 'Name Changes' because these were all crucial elements in one man's story. Some themes such as migration, a war, natural disaster or a criminal conviction may need to feature prominently due to the impact they had on your ancestors' lives and those of their descendants. How much emphasis you give these will be influenced by your own personal interests or something that catches your imagination, as was the case with the history of duelling in England I included in one family history.

Background context does not have to be nationally important. It can be any event that causes change; interrupts everyday life; or impacts on people, such as a harvest supper or bad winter. For instance, I used the terrible winter and agricultural depression of 1816 when talking about someone who lived at that time. Whilst I have no idea what the person I was writing about experienced or thought, there are a number of contemporary accounts from newspapers and diaries from which I could quote. This is an instance where modern knowledge can add another dimension to writing, as it would be relevant to explain this bad weather was probably caused by a volcanic eruption in Indonesia in 1815.

Tip

- Create a prompt list of events you want to include and who they relate to. If you already have specific details then just make bullet points or write a very brief outline of each event and the actual or likely impact it had on an ancestor. For example:

  Event A) Bad winter 1816 (cause: volcanic eruption).
  Effects: poor harvest, economic depression.
  Likely impact on John: reduced living standards and lack of food.
  Theories: Might explain move and change of job.

Exercise

Having some idea of the number of themes to be included and their length will help you decide on how your history needs to be structured. The following is a useful aid in deciding on whether, when and where to add in sub-headings, sidebars or separate chapters.

- Create two columns on a page and make a list of all the themes you want to write about relating to one ancestor in one. For example, their jobs, a particular time period, hobbies, or places lived.
- In the other column list whether this is likely to be a short piece – less than a page or two – or a long piece of over two pages (guess if you are not sure).

Writing Plan

Now that you have considered what and who to include, as well as your style, format and other important considerations, it is time to start putting it into practice. Create a writing plan now if you have not already done so. If you already have a plan, see if it needs refining. Review this plan regularly and tick off what has been achieved as well as noting any particular problems that need resolving. To give you an idea, here is the first rough plan I created for a book on the history of my Marris ancestors. In it you can see I include my aims, format, deadlines and some practical questions.

Writing Plan for the Marris Family of Lincolnshire
What do I want to produce and what will it look like?
- Book of one family line with chapters for each generation.
- Introduction – summarising where I've got to, what is missing and any questions.
- Appendices – list of sources, outline of research process, explanation of terminology, extra information.

Deadlines/aims
- Finish whole project in time for a family gathering.
- Aim – how many hours or words a day/week/month?
- Mini deadlines – first generation to be written within two months, second generation within another two months – draft ready exactly one year from start.
- Who will proofread?
- Revision and editing – three months.
- Rewards (self-bribery) for every mini goal and deadline achieved (I personally favour chocolate, wine, a meal out or money in a piggy bank).

What else will be in it?
- Copies of documents (check copyright), family trees, timelines.

What do I know?
- Back to late 1700s.

Additional research required – time needed, locations, when to stop?
- Can I take it any further?
- Details of female lines?
- What happened to children?

Places to visit/where to get information (and when)
- Record offices and family history societies.
- Museums.

- Online – village histories.
- Visit – summer time.

Exercise

Try creating your own writing plan on one or two sides of a page (no more). One method is to write it as if it was a contents page.

- List who you are going to write about.
- Make a brief note of key events and turning points essential to the story. Focus on the how and why, such as occupations, illegitimacy or migration.
- List any further research needed and where to find it.
- Draft a timetable broken down into phases (see the section on time management on pp. 34–36).
- Once you have done some experimenting with your format and voice and have decided on what to include, look at your plan again and see if anything needs to be added or changed.

Starting to Write

Now you have made a plan it is time to start writing. Try some of these writing exercises to get going. You may also find them useful if you get stuck and when starting a new stage of writing.

- Pick five people from your ancestry and write a one-sentence description for each of them.
- Write a 500-word biography of a relative or ancestor in the third person.
- Write your own obituary as if it were someone else you have always admired. List all your life's accomplishments as bullet points first. Then expand these into short sentences. A useful tip from author Simon Fowler is to look at the *Oxford Dictionary of National Biography* (DNB) for examples of how to write concise biographies that include every essential point (www.oxforddnb.com). The DNB can be accessed free from home via most library services.
- Write a one-paragraph description of one room in your house.
- Describe a favourite place – where was it, why was it special and can you remember any sounds or smells?
- Pick one event in an ancestor's life and describe who they were and what was happening. This can be either in the past or present tense.
- Take a historical event such as the Blitz, Nelson's death, women voting for the first time or children no longer being able to work down mines.

Now write a short piece about this event in a way that includes one of your ancestors.

- Describe a smell, colour or sound in no more than two sentences.
- Use that description as part of a piece about one event in your family history. For example, the smell of newly mown hay as the harvest is brought in, or unwashed bodies crammed together in a workhouse dormitory.
- Write a short piece about the birth, marriage or death of one of your ancestors in the manner of a news report.
- Find a travel or historical description of a place associated with your family history. Now put it into your own words.
- Select an image relating to your ancestry such as a portrait, painting, photograph or map. Describe it as if you were on the phone to someone who cannot see it.
- Now envisage this same image as if it were a film. Describe what happens in the next scene.
- Pick an aspect of your family history, set an alarm for 10 minutes and just keep writing about it for the whole time.
- Now expand that to 20 minutes for another aspect.

Exercise
- Draw up a list of all the jobs an ancestor had.
- Write down all the places they lived.
- Add a list of people they knew through work or leisure.
- Note any hobbies or interests.
- Write down the names, jobs and interests of people they knew. For example, 'Edwin Blanchard, rat catcher, worked for the Ministry of Agriculture. Liked to restore old farm machinery. Born in Cliffe, Yorkshire. Lived in Skipton, Beverley and Horsham, Sussex (retirement home). People: a) Wife Maisie; b) Sister Eleanor keen piano player, artist and poetess; c) Brother-in-law a local farmer; d) Sister Margaret wrote poems in dialect'.
- Take these notes and write a short biography of that person just using the notes you have made. Do not worry if your information is incomplete, it can be expanded on later.

Exercise
- Write your autobiography in 50 to 100 words maximum.
- Now do the same for your each of your siblings.
- Then add your mother and father and their siblings.
- Follow with your grandparents and their siblings.

Chapter 2

WHEN TO STOP RESEARCHING

There will always be questions left unanswered and 'missing' ancestors to be found. Writing a family history therefore means accepting your research will never be finished and deciding to do it anyway.

You can either stop researching completely. Or, and this is more common, identify areas that need additional research whilst starting to write. This could be anything from occupations and how people travelled to the cost of food. If you set clear limits on how much extra research you will do it should not be an obstacle to writing. Writing instalments on particular individuals or generations is a very effective strategy to solve this problem as it allows you to start writing whilst continuing to research. Any major new findings can then be produced in a sequel.

Dave wondered if it was time to stop researching.

If you stop your research in stages then it is advisable to set deadlines and goals to do the research in so that the writing does not get put to one side. Part of your preparation should be to identify any additional background research that may be needed. What I did with my Marris and Ismay ancestors was to set myself a list of research goals that could be achieved within a certain time period and set a budget to spend on it. Once I had completed that I would write about the research I had done in the foreword or an appendix and explain any gaps or aspects not followed up on. The 'unknowns' would almost certainly get mentioned again as part of the story in the relevant sections of the family history.

Tip

- If you think of something you need to conduct research on whilst writing just make a note of it and carry on with the writing. One of my methods is to make a note in the middle of what I am writing so as to not disturb the flow. I do this by using square brackets and putting my note to myself in bold or a coloured font. Often, these are in the form of questions with the prefix 'CHECK'.

Exercise

- Make a check list of the additional research you absolutely feel is a must.
- Create a timetable of when to do this research with dates and proposed lengths of time.
- Keep this with list you when you are writing and add to it as needed.

How Much Time to Write a Family History?

I wrote one family history in a month whilst another took over two years. Obviously the amount of time it takes will vary enormously according to the amount of information that needs to be included and how much time you can devote to it. Nevertheless, it can be useful to get an idea of what is possible physically by working out how many words you should aim at daily, weekly or monthly.

The average length of the family history books I write is 20,000 to 40,000 words. Let us assume you are going to allow a year for a book totalling 30,000 words. Divide this figure by months, weeks and days and it is 2,500 words a month, just under 600 a week and just over 82 a day. Whether it is a book, website or series of blogs add in extra time for proofreading, editing and layout and some leeway for holidays, sickness and unexpected interruptions. Even if all you wrote was 100 to 200 words a day, you would easily finish a family history in that time.

Tips

- Set a word target for each writing session. Say, 500, 1,000 or 2,000 words. Stop when you reach it. If you have time left over use it for reviewing something you have already written or making notes so that you can go back to the piece you have just finished with fresh eyes after a short break.
- Try writing for 15 minutes or half an hour every day for a week. Then gradually increase.

Deadlines and Goals

Deadlines force you to complete each stage of your project. The goal here is to get each piece done within a specified time frame. Revising and polishing can always be done later. The best way to meet these deadlines is to schedule writing time, just as you would a visit to the doctor or hairdresser.

Deadlines can be a good thing. There is nothing like a looming deadline to make you focus and get a move on. It can influence the pace and tone of what you write by making your text short and snappy instead of long and meandering. Sometimes you have to adjust your targets simply because they are unrealistic or events happen over which you have no control. What you do have control over is your attitude. If you decide to reschedule your deadline, do so positively and see it as an opportunity to complete your writing in the way you want.

Tips

- Create short-term deadlines for different stages such as writing a chapter on one generation or an interlude on local history and put this in your diary.
- Base this deadline on how much time you can give to writing each week and assume there will be unexpected interruptions. Do not forget time to proofread.
- Promise yourself rewards and treats when you meet each goal.

Time and Space

Time management is not something that comes naturally to many people (myself included). There may be practical and/or financial factors that influence how we spend time outside of work and caring for family, but very few people in the Western World have absolutely no spare time at all. Creating that time and space does however mean being realistic. It is better to settle for less than an ideal than to try and fail to do more. If you only have half an hour a day then use it. Many writers find that working within limited time constraints is a positive experience in that it forces one to be disciplined and focused.

It is the easiest thing in the world to find excuses not to write. If you need help with organising your time there are numerous guides available in print or online. One of the most useful techniques I adopted when a mature student fitting study in around family life is to draw up a weekly timetable that includes everything from work, leisure, study, housework, travel, holidays, reading and sleep in blocks of time. Include whether time spent travelling on a bus or train or sitting in a waiting room can be usefully employed in something to do with your writing. Block out set chunks of time for your writing on this timetable, whether is 20 minutes or 2 hours. Creating a physical timetable in this way not only prepares you psychologically for writing, but allows you to see whether your chosen slots work practically.

Tips

- Schedule writing days and times in your diary. If something prevents you from writing then make sure you schedule a replacement session.
- Get up half an hour or an hour earlier every day in order to work. Delay watching television or other evening leisure activities by an hour and spend the time writing.
- Consciously choose to make time limitations work for you by focusing on aspects that need a shorter, sharper, more urgent tone to them. For example, describing a busy work place or a railway journey.

Exercises

- Keep a writing diary.
- Plan your first month's writing timetable, setting aside a certain time every week or day. Put these days and times in your diary. Reschedule your writing times if something interferes, but do not let them just disappear.
- At the end of each week tick off the time you spent writing and the number of words and pages written. Check whether it matched your goals. If not, consider why not and whether your goals need to be adjusted.
- Note anything that stopped you from writing and whether it was a one-off or likely to be a regular event. If the latter, consider how you can stop it happening or adjust your schedule accordingly.
- Be positive and celebrate any specific writing goals reached.
- Check your revised list just before you start writing again so it is fresh

in your mind. Tick off each task when it is accomplished. Review it at the end of each session and refresh it again if needed.

- Finally, list any particular problems you had with the writing itself and create an action plan to resolve it. This might be as simple as adding a note to your existing writing plan or having a separate 'problem' list.

Tips – Writing Friends

- Arrange to work with someone else at a set day and time each week. For this to work effectively you have to agree a timetable in advance. This might take the following form. Meeting at 1pm you spend 10 minutes making tea or coffee and exchanging writing news. This should focus on any additions, ideas or discoveries relating to your project since you last met. You might add in 5 minutes to discuss what you plan to work on during this session and what you want to achieve. At a set time – 1.15pm for example – you settle down and start writing. You might even be in separate rooms. Do not worry if you are at different stages.
- At a time agreed in advance stop writing and either summarise what you have done, take it in turns to read a piece of work out loud or give it to each other to read and be critiqued. If you do not want to share what you have written then describe what you have done such as the number of words written, whether you met that day's goals, what point you have got to overall and what you will work on next.

A Room of Your Own

We cannot all have a room of our own, hours to spare or the option to avoid other people when writing. It is easy to be put off from starting to write by external and inner voices that say you must write in isolation, silence and at the same time each day or week. If all that is available to you is a corner of the sofa for a few hours each week then that is what works for you. Designating a space and time to write in even if you are surrounded by people will encourage others to respect that space. Tell people this is what you are doing. Create a large sign that says 'WRITING DO NOT DISTURB' and pin it to your back if necessary.

Try using your local library or a cafe. Try meeting up with other writers or giving up your lunch hour, setting aside time in the morning before others get up or after they have gone to bed at night. I frequently write, proofread or edit on trains, buses, park benches, in libraries, restaurants, waiting rooms and even the pub (although perhaps not as eloquently as I thought at the time). Although I prefer to use a computer, I can still be found scribbling in notebooks and on scraps of paper when needs must. In short,

Do you think this counts as the house being on fire?

the message is to work where you can. One of my students looked after her grandchildren before and after school a couple of days a week. She arranged with her daughter that she would stay at her daughter's house in between on at least one of those days to write away from any distractions at home.

Other Planning Points

Part of your plan should include notes about your strengths and weaknesses as a writer such as being good at condensing facts or imaginative, or not being able to describe places or people. Again, make a note of these and use the tips and exercises in Chapter 4, 'Make it Interesting', as problem-solving tools.

Chapter 3

DEVELOPING WRITING SKILLS

Your family's story deserves to be told in a way that would interest even the most casual reader. There is no good reason why a family history cannot be as interesting as any other form of literature. Yet many are little more than lists. What transforms a set of words into captivating reading is the quality of writing and scene setting as much as content.

Good writing techniques can be applied to every type of writing from fiction to scientific. This chapter looks at some of the techniques used by novelists to tell a gripping story, set compelling scenes, bring characters to life and portray their surroundings and lives. This is achieved through believable characters; convincing background; good openings; pace, tension; a coherent sense of shape; strong characterisation and imagery; a sense of time and place and a satisfying ending. These make the reader want to know more about the people and events even if they are not related to them. With family histories the characters and events in their lives are the plot and it is the way we present those factors and how we write that creates pace and so on.

Tips
- Start by making a simple list of key events about a particular person or event then go back and start writing them as sentences and paragraphs.
- Think about the reaction you want your reader to have to an ancestor's circumstances, personality and actions. It is not enough simply to say that someone was humorous, careful with money, kind or cruel. The reader needs to see, feel and believe that through the language you use.

Exercise
- Pick a good author or book you like and analyse what elements of their writing style you would like yours to emulate.
- Break down how and why by noting specific elements that grabs you such as vivid imagery or interweaving of narratives.
- Take one section or chapter and note how the author does this and what makes it unique or identifiable. This might be a particular tone

of voice or distinctive phrasing – cool, passionate, breathy or measured for instance. It might be the narrative structure where the writer starts with an event before going back in time, or the use of specific details that make their background come alive.

- List ways in which you might use similar techniques in your own work.

All skills improve through practice so get in the habit of writing regularly even if you feel uninspired. Even the clunkiest of sentences or a simple list of ideas can be improved and rewritten, but a blank page cannot. Many writers make themselves write regularly at set times or up to a certain number of words regardless of whether they feel inspired or they start with free writing to warm up – writing against the clock without worrying about sentence structure, grammar or punctuation. Once something is on the page it can then be reshaped and polished. Writing under this kind of pressure can force you to focus on the essential points you want to make and how it might be presented and frees you from your inner editor/critic.

Exercise

- Pick an ancestor or event at random. Don't spend any time on trying to choose. If you can't choose, list three or four names or events and stick a pin in. Do not change your mind.
- Set an alarm to go off after 5 or 10 minutes.
- Now write about that person or event from memory without stop until the alarm goes off.
- Now look at how you can expand and refine it.

Dialogue

As mentioned in Chapter 1, family histories do not tend to have much dialogue unless they are fictionalised or quoting from original source material. Where it is used dialogue needs to be fast paced with no unnecessary words or descriptions. To do this, the family historian has to find a balance between retaining accuracy and engaging their reader.

Although it is wonderful to get a sense of how one of our ancestors spoke and thought there is a tendency when quoting from documents to repeat every word. This is rarely necessary. Instead, choose carefully so as to make every quotation and word spoken really stand out and provide a flavour of the language used and attitudes of the time. Transcripts of the full accounts can always be included in an appendix for those who do want to read everything. As an example, in one piece I wrote I used selections of people's own words from diaries, letters, memoirs and oral histories. Rather than simply quoting them directly as a 'he said, she said', I wove as many as possible into the story. For example:

> As Roger Martin remained in India the Burnham Westgate villagers celebrated the Allies entering Paris with roasted ox, fireworks and 'eating jelly off plates in Holkham Park, or humble plum pudding in the Market Place at Burnham, but always ending with a dance'. News came of Napoleon escaping from Elba, then 'glorious victory' at Waterloo in 1815. This was followed in 1816 by 'great commercial and agricultural distress', as Elizabeth Jones and other local ladies distributed 'the most capital soup' to relieve the suffering of the poor. (All quotations from: 'Reminiscences of Elizabeth Jones, 1801–1866' at: www.jjhc.info/joneselizabeth1866diary.htm.)

Tips

- Be aware that writing speech exactly as it is spoken does not work on the page as people's conversations meander, they hesitate, say 'um' and 'ah', interrupt and repeat themselves.
- Too much information in speech makes a character sound false so keep it brief.
- Make each voice as distinctive as possible so that it is always clear who is speaking. This does not need to be complicated. A simple 'he said, she said' will do.

Even without dialogue you can convey a flavour of how someone might have spoken through phrasing and relevant references. Try saying something like: 'despite spending most of her adult life in Kent Mary retained her Northumberland burr'. This could then be followed by examples of Northumberland words and phrases passed on to descendants.

Exercises

- Look at a range of stories you like and note how they present speech. See what pauses occur, how it switches from one person to another, whether there is a change of tone and so on. Now consciously apply that structure to something you want your characters to say.
- Record two people having an ordinary conversation for 5 minutes (don't forget to ask permission first).
- Transcribe it exactly as it is heard.
- Now re-write that conversation as if it were two of your ancestors talking, cutting out what is unnecessary and keeping what might move a story on.

- Read it aloud and hear how it works.

Feedback and Motivation

Stories are crafted, polished and presented. The story of my grandfather only wanting to eat porridge when he was young is not an interesting fact in itself. The key to making such a fact appeal to a wider audience would be to tell it in a manner that provides a real glimpse into his personality. Even the most experienced writer hones these skills over time. Many do so by learning from other writers and having their work critiqued through writing courses, writers' circles and online forums. If you wish to work specifically with people who share your interest in family history then set up a group by advertising in a local family history society and on online forums.

Joining a reading or book group is a great way of discovering the craft of effective writing through analysing and deconstructing other people's work. The knowledge of what works for us as readers can then be applied practically to our own writing. You can find details of local writing or reading groups via your library service. There are many creative writing courses and workshops run through adult education, local universities, the Open University and other organisations. Whilst many of these are focused on fiction or poetry they can still prove invaluable.

There are some courses and workshops that specialise in historical, biographical and genealogical writing including the MA in Biography and Creative Non Fiction at the University of East Anglia and my own courses and workshops on Writing Your Family History at the Society of Genealogists, online at www.writingyourfamilyhistory.com and elsewhere.

The Writers' Centre in Norwich is being developed into a national writing centre (www.writerscentrenorwich.org.uk). The Arvon Foundation for Writing encourages writing of all kinds, including non-fiction, through its four writing centres and numerous groups and courses across the country (www.arvon.org). The Ways With Words organisation offers writing holidays in the UK and abroad (www.wayswithwords.co.uk). There are a huge number of online writing forums where you can share your work, writing problems and get feedback. Again, many are focused on fiction, but are still well worth a look. Wattpad (www.wattpad.com) for instance is a mobile reading app that encourages writers to share their work. A useful umbrella website with links to courses and resources for writers is writersforum (www.writersforum.co.uk).

Tips

- Enter competitions, submit to anthologies or write something for a manuscript evening at a writing event. Entering competitions and following their guidelines enables you to start processing your own data. Even if you are not planning a fictionalised account you will undoubtedly be able to use some of it in a more factual project. National writing magazines such as *Writers' Forum* (www.writers-forum.com; this has the same name but is not the website listed above) and *Writing Magazine* (www.writers-online.co.uk) list competitions and other writing challenges, whilst there are a growing number online.

- Get out of home and try writing in cafes, libraries, museums, art galleries, the park or garden. J.K. Rowling didn't just write in cafes because she was saving on heating bills (you still have to buy a drink). Stepping away from home formalises the permission we give ourselves to set aside time to write, whilst different sounds, sights and smells can stimulate creativity. A visit to a museum before settling down in their cafe has the added bonus of providing historical and social context.
- Ask people who have no knowledge of family history biographies or research to read your writing and tell you what works or does not work for them.

Exercises
- Take a short piece from something you have already written.
- Rewrite the first one or two paragraphs in the same style as an author you admire.
- Now 'free write' the rest of it without reading what you wrote before.
- Compare the two versions and note what you do and don't like and why.
- Give the two versions to someone else to read and ask for feedback.

Become a Literary Critic
One of the most useful writing tips I ever had was to write reviews of other people's work looking closely at format, style and structure rather than focusing specifically on content. Analyse work of those you admire, particularly in the fields of biography, history and historical fiction. This type of analysis involves looking closely at what it is that grips you, how they convey excitement and where and when they place defining or dramatic moments. Perhaps even more pertinent for family historians is to look at how authors convey a sense a drama and pace where there is not much action. Questions to consider are whether 'interest' is brought in from outside through description and background detail for instance.

By reading critically you can assess the elements of what makes good story and apply it to your own. Taking *Angela's Ashes* and *'Tis* (Harper Perennial, 2005) by Frank McCourt as an example, these are acclaimed as fascinating memoirs of life in Ireland in the first half of the twentieth century. Yet, his family were probably no more interesting than any other living in Limerick in this period. McCourt's experiences come to life in the way they are presented so that we see and feel what he did.

The next level is to write reviews of other people's work. This kind of deconstruction involves looking at format, style and structure rather than focusing specifically on content. Questions to consider when reviewing include whether certain sections would work better placed elsewhere, was it clear when things happened and why and how people were introduced. Look at whether the characterisation is believable for that place, time or social class. Think about whether you felt as if you 'knew' a place mentioned and if so, why and how was that feeling conveyed. Was it through the wording, type of language used, quotes from authentic sources or images for instance?

Finally, ask yourself why you wanted to keep reading, or what is it that made you stop. You may not be able to answer or see anything obvious immediately, but getting in the habit of this kind of analysis will feed into your own writing both directly and indirectly.

Exercise

- Choose a chapter from a book or an article you like. If you can't find a family history then choose a history, historical fiction, memoir or biography.
- Outline its structure. Is it chronological, flashback, thematic or from different viewpoints?
- Note what you like about it and what you don't like and why.
- List up to five ways in which it could be improved, for example, less terminology, clearer chronology or more explanation.
- Now take at least one of those points and note how this improvement could be made practically such as moving a piece of text or adding or taking something out.
- If you are feeling adventurous try rewriting one of these sections you have critiqued using one or more of your ideas for improvement as if it were your own work. Once done review it again and ask others for their feedback on how it works.
- Now be prepared to do the same with your own work.

Exercise

- Look at a selection of reviews of historical and biographical books in newspapers and magazines. Include essays in publications such as the *London Review of Books* (www.lrb.co.uk), *History Today* (www.historytoday.com), *BBC History Magazine* (www.historyextra.com) and the *Journal of the British Association for Local History* (BALH). The BALH website has many reviews freely available online at www.balh.co.uk/tlh.

- Make a note of what aspects the reviewers focus on. You will see most, if not all, comment on how a piece is structured, the style of writing, how it is presented, the depth and clarity of arguments or research as well as how readable it is.
- Check whether there is a 'house style', i.e. if reviews for particular publications follow an identifiable format and who they use to write them.
- See what the average length each review is (one I wrote recently for a magazine was just 200 words).
- Think about what it is in each review that either encourages you to read the item being reviewed or puts you off.
- Write out some of the most pertinent phrases the reviewers use when critiquing. Now rewrite them into your own words and add similar phrases of your own.
- Using this list as a guide, write reviews of a selection of other people's writings as if you had been commissioned by a magazine or newspaper.

Start as You Mean to Go On – 'the Hook'

Grab your reader's attention right from the beginning. Making an impact in every new chapter or section will keep them reading. Start positive and celebrate your achievement in creating this history. Particular events, questions, mysteries and quotations can create a sense of drama.

Good examples of great opening chapters include the family memoirs *Angela's Ashes* by Frank McCourt (Harper Perennial, 2005), *Bad Blood* by Lorna Sage (Fourth Estate, 2000) and Kate Atkinson's fictionalised family history *Behind the Scenes at the Museum* (Black Swan, 1998). Even a simple statement about why this ancestral tale begins where it does can be given weight through careful phrasing and a hint of what is to come. Your audience already wants to know more so let them know upfront what an interesting and exciting journey they are about to undertake. Neither does a family history have to start at the beginning with the earliest known ancestor or be cradle to grave. Instead, consider starting with a pivotal moment, a character forming event or change in circumstances, then writing about what led up to it.

The next stage is to link episodes in a life or different generations. Set limits to each episode, such as childhood and work experiences or one generation at a time. Write them up separately then link them together. If possible, describe significant events such as a birth, marriage, death, a house move or change of job, etc. Focusing on an important episode allows you to look back at what happened before, and forward to what would happen next.

Tips

- I often start a piece of writing with relevant quotations or a copy of a document with an accompanying extract. This has the double advantage of allowing comparisons and comments to be made about social, legal or political changes that have occurred over time.
- A story of someone's life does not have to start with their birth. A great method of grabbing the reader's interest is to start a narrative with an interesting fact, record or quote. You can then fill the reader in on the events which lead up to your opening story.

Exercises

- Pick out an interesting aspect from your family history and deliberately start a piece of writing with it.
- Look at whether this draws you in and how it might change the shape of the narrative.
- Take an opening you like from a story. Pick one from a family history, biography or historical fiction so that it is as close to the family history genre as possible.
- Write the first paragraph out and analyse what it is that drew you in.
- Now write the beginning of your piece in the same style and compare the two for effectiveness.

Be Positive

Too many family histories use negative statements. Think about what news items catch your eye when reading a newspaper. If you stop to analyse them you will almost certainly see that they are couched in a dramatic and positive (some might say 'strong') manner. This is because we respond to the build-up, the idea that we are about to go on a journey or discover something.

'I have only traced my Marris ancestry back to the late 1700s'. Consider your reaction when you read this and whether you really want to find out more. I suspect most people would wonder if it is worth bothering to continue because the writer has 'only' got so far. The reader will subconsciously focus on the word 'only'. This implies a sense of failure or lack of effort (undoubtedly untrue) and encourages the reader to focus on what you have not done and what is missing.

'I don't know'. Do you want to read more now? I doubt it. There is hardly a more negative statement to start with, so don't. Even though there will be times when a lack of knowledge has to be revealed this can be done later. As in fiction, you will draw your reader in if you start positive and celebrate your achievement in creating this history. For example: 'The history of the Marris family can be traced back to the late 1700s'. Or, 'this story of the Ismay family begins in the 1700s'.

Tip
- A useful technique is to go through your work with a red pen and mark every negative or weak statement. Then consciously change those identified to something stronger and more assertive.

Show Not Tell

'Show not tell' is one of the most common catchphrases in creative writing. This is because 'showing' a reader how and why something happened rather than simply describing it is the most effective method of drawing them into a story. In doing so we enable our readers to come as close as possible to touching, smelling, seeing and hearing what went on in our ancestors' lives, without tipping over into fantasy. Showing the reader their lives involves using an active voice as much as possible so as to be 'present' with the moment.

This can be done through empathy, drawing on our own experiences to make comparisons, recreating a scene or 'feel' through images and descriptions of scenery and buildings. At the same time it can be tricky to get the balance right so as not to overdo descriptions of places, weather or scenery.

Tip
- Try speaking directly through the material you have rather than just describing it. If you have a marriage entry for instance, don't just say 'Miles Camplejohn married Mary Abbott on November 18th 1707'. Instead tell your reader it was winter, how far they travelled, what day of the week it was, what the church was like and so on. Make them see what is happening. This might go something like: 'Just six weeks before Christmas 1707, the small church on the top of the hill was the setting for the wedding of Miles Camplejohn and Mary Abbott'.

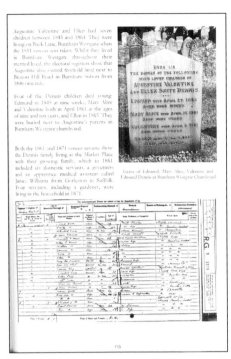
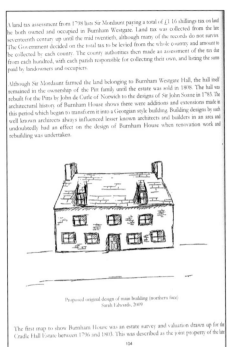

Examples 'showing' not 'telling' by integrating documents and drawings.

It is important to use an active voice wherever possible. This means helping the reader experience the past more directly. Show them how a loom worked and what it was it was like to go down into a mine for work. Think about how to tell others how and why an ancestor moved from one place to another. Simply stating that someone was listed at different places on the census returns is 'telling' the reader. Combining copies of those census returns with an account of what such a move entailed is more active.

Instead of just stating that my Blanchard ancestors came from a long line of wheelwrights and carpenters in Barlby in Yorkshire, I looked for pictures of wheelwrights and descriptions of their day-to-day life in the late nineteenth century. I found one about a George Stuart of Farnham in Surrey in a wonderful book, John Burnett (ed.)'s *Useful Toil: Autobiographies of Working People from the 1820s to the 1920s* (Penguin, 1974 and Kindle, 2013). This is a collection of biographical and auto-biographical accounts of working class people's working lives from the nineteenth and twentieth centuries. Putting it into your own words by paraphrasing is equally effective and avoids copyright issues from using published material. Although it was from a different county many of the practices and experiences would have been the same so I integrated quotes such as the following.

> The business I started into in 1884 was old fashioned . . . it was a 'folk' industry, carried on in the 'folk' method . . . Farmers rarely more than five miles away; millers, brewers, a local grocer or builder or timber-merchant or hop-grower – for such and no others did the ancient shop still cater, as it had done for nearly two centuries . . . A good wheelwright knew by art but not by reasoning the proportion to keep between spokes and felloes . . . He felt it, in his bones.

Tips
- Include copies of the documents such as census returns.
- Use the words and written accounts of real people about their work, travel, poverty, married lives and so on to create a more active and direct experience.

Drama and Tension
Everybody has turning points or dramatic moments in their lives, which on the surface, may not seem worthy of public attention. Our challenge as writers is to make our readers care that about our ancestors' day-to-day lives. Doing so means enabling our readers to experience it as directly as possible. This is the 'who, what, where, when, why and how' that underpins all stories. To make a crime-novel analogy, this means that the places where my ancestors lived and their occupations are either clues or background plot that give the reader important information, but allows them to become mentally involved by putting the pieces together themselves.

Each piece of writing should drive the reader on by making them want to know how something happened, why it occurred and what comes next (the what). In the case of my Marris family the how and why would be their migration from the north to the south of England. The consequences of that move are what happened next. This means that there is an ebb and flow to the narrative with all the relevant details linked together.

Exercise
- Identify a key turning point in your family history and decide where it is likely to be placed in your story, i.e. the beginning of a chapter, the middle or end.
- Now, write a short description of what happened. For example, when writing about the Marris family who moved from Northumberland to Kent in the mid-1850s this might go something like: 'In the 1850s, the

Marris family, with all their worldly goods, journeyed over 300 miles from Northumberland to a new home in Kent'.

- An alternative version is: 'The Marris family spent days, possibly weeks, moving all their worldly goods from Northumberland to their new home in Kent'. Immediately, the focus is on the move and what it involved, which creates natural drama and sense of tension, albeit quite small. We don't have a why or how (yet), but there is a 'who (Marris family), what (moving, journey and goods), where (counties) and when (mid-1850s)'.
- Now, re-write your chosen event in a more active and dramatic manner as in the example given only using known facts.
- Look again at where you plan to place this event and think about how you will build up to this event from preceding ones, or how you can use it to lead onto something else so that each piece drives the reader on, wanting to know more.

Pace

Pace is what gives a piece of writing 'oomph'. It underpins the facts and chronology by propelling readers through all those details. To use an analogy, your family history can be compared to a railway line that takes you from A to B. Pace is the train journey; its speed; length; number of stops; delays; diversions and so on. It is what gives your tale momentum. To continue the analogy, it can create frustration or confusion in the person travelling (reading) because things do not progress in a satisfactory manner. At its worst, the traveller gives up on reaching their destination, or, in this case, your lovingly created family history is unread or unfinished. At its most basic level 'pace' simply means the rhythm, speed or rate of progression through which the elements of the story are gradually exposed.

It is how and where you set up events or introduce a character that creates pace and a story out of a mass of detail. In crime stories a typical pattern is the uncovering of clues, evidence and motives ending with the criminal being discovered or brought to justice, whilst in a romance the star-crossed lovers achieve happiness after many trials and tribulations. This can be tricky to achieve in family histories where some or all of what happens in the story is already known to the reader. For us, it is the turning points, key events and personal developments in our ancestors' lives that become the central force in creating a lively and varied pace.

Tips

- A common writing tip is to open a book you like at random and copy out a couple of paragraphs. Then do the same with two or three other books. This gives you a physical sense of how the writing was built up and a feel for its rhythm.

- Consciously vary the length of your sentences to change pace. Several short sentences followed by a long one will sub-consciously refocus a reader's attention. Some authors deliberately change their sentence length to correspond with a major change in the text. In a family history this might be a birth, marriage, death or other important event.

Themes and interludes have been mentioned in Chapter 1 in relation to organising information. They do however have crucial roles to play in creating drama, tension and changes of pace. The change of pace occurs once you switch from a piece of genealogical information to a specific aspect of their lives such as where they live, the impact of a war, personality traits and particular skills. As these layers are built up the rhythm of the writing will change, even if only slightly, as the focus shifts between events or on to memorabilia such as photographs, jewellery, clothes, paintings, recipes and letters.

Tip

- When focusing on the main line in each generation makes sure you keep the focus on them. If you introduce other characters or events you must take care not to let this supporting cast swamp the story.

Exercise

- Start by writing out the relationships between 2 sets of relatives or 1 fact in no more than 200 words.
- Once done, read it aloud even if only to yourself. Whilst doing so listen out for whether it makes sense, is clear and interesting. Note down the areas that need working on and any ideas you have on how to do so.
- Don't forget to note the aspects you are pleased with.

The first family history piece I wrote was about my maternal grandmother, Norah Naughton (née Guerin). First of all, I simply wrote the facts I knew about her life, my memories and stories I had heard from relatives. This was only a few sides of A4. Then I showed it to my mother, who gave me more information. I added this in and then found local history material for places where she was born and lived. I used this to expand the piece I had already written by summarising the general history and quoting from people's oral histories and memories. The end result was considerably longer than the first short piece I wrote. Yet, if I had set out to write something that long I would probably have given up at the start. I then moved on to write about other family members separately. At the end I had a series of booklets.

As well as expanding our ancestors' lives from snippets, we face the task of how to present complicated and detailed information to others. This might be how we came to prove particular relationships, describe a series of historical events, explain technical terms or what someone did as part of their job. The problem lies in providing essential information without overloading the reader. The key is often to keep it simple and short, but allow room to expand on anything particularly relevant more fully.

Tips

- A good technique for producing short, sharp relevant pieces is to condense a large mass of information into a handout of no more than two to four sides. It should include key events and have a coherent structure, i.e. a beginning, middle and end. Once done you should have all the essential detail you need. You can then expand it into a fully written piece once more, but limit it to no more than double the size the handout is.
- Explain something from your family history as if you were writing for an 8- or 9-year-old, or someone who does not speak very good English.
- Swap the item you need to simplify with someone else. You write theirs and they write yours to a set word limit.

Exercise

This is a variation on using timelines as a framework for writing.

- Ancestor 1: Take their age at death and divide it roughly by six time periods on a page. So if they lived to the age of 90 each time period will be fifteen years in length, whereas someone who only lived to the age of 35 will have time periods of around five-and-half or six years.
- Within those time lines list major events in their lives such as births and deaths, house moves, school changes, jobs or travel.
- If you are a visual person then you can do the same using graphs, diagrams or spidergraphs.
- Pick one of these events and write no more than a paragraph on it.
- Once this is done choose another event to write about.
- Once you have written three or four pieces see if you can link these events together chronologically. You may need to add in a link sentence so it makes sense, but other than that do not make any changes.

- Now make notes about which aspects you want to expand and where to put in images.

Exercise

- Part one of this exercise is to start with a simple list of key events for that person or event. For example:
  i) John Smith was born in 1837.
  ii) John married Mary Jones on 5 May 1860.
  iii) Mary Jones was born in 1838.
  iv) John and Mary Smith had five children, all born in Norfolk.

- Part two is to turn these facts into sentences. For example:
  John Smith was born in 1837. Victoria had just become queen. John married his sweetheart Mary Jones on 5 May 1860 at the age of 23. Mary was 22 years old and the daughter of William Jones, a railway worker. Together they had five children born in Norfolk, all of whom survived childhood.

- Part three is to rewrite those sentences into paragraphs by adding more detail about where these people lived and worked.

There are other techniques for linking episodes in a life or different generations. One is to write out each individual episode separately. If possible, describe significant events such as a birth, marriage, death, house move or change of job, etc. Focusing on an important episode allows you to look back at what happened before, and forward to what would happen next.

Exercise

- Pick five people from your ancestry and write a one-sentence description of each of them. If you do not know what they looked like then use an event, family trait or characteristic they shared.
- Now add underneath five facts or family stories such as date and place of birth, a job or hobbies, address they lived in or people they knew.
- Link the description, characteristic or first fact you wrote to one of those written underneath and turn it into a paragraph. As far as possible describe any other people involved in that event as well as what happened.

In the example that follows I have used the family story that my grandfather Ted Blanchard's birth date was registered incorrectly. Rather than just say what was supposed to have happened I try to bring in some ideas of how it might have occurred. Alternatively, this could be elaborated on to make more of a story by adding details such as how Ted knew and information on the birth registration process and home births generally.

Edwin (Ted) Blanchard was born in Cliffe in Yorkshire at the end of October 1905 to Robert and Isabelle Blanchard (née Marris). It was a home birth as was the norm at this time. A father might be in the house when his wife was in labour, but rarely attended the birth itself. This was left to a midwife and any other female helpers available. For a family with limited financial means a doctor would only be called in if there were major problems, and perhaps not even then.

Ted always claimed his father Robert had put down the wrong date as a consequence of getting drunk whilst celebrating the birth of his first son after four girls. The home birth meant no officials in attendance to fill in paperwork and the registrar had no reason to question the information given. We can only speculate as to when Belle discovered the mistake and whether cost played a part in why Ted's birth certificate was never corrected.

Tip

- Keep a notebook with you in which you can jot down notes, reminders, flashes of inspiration or instructions on where and how to move a piece of text. Reading, watching television or visiting a place might for instance give you an idea about how to build in a piece of local history or an interesting method to add copies of artwork, poetry or music. Write up those notes and follow those instructions as soon as you possibly can.

Practicalities

Spelling, Grammar and Punctuation

Grammar and punctuation are important in order for the reader to understand what you are saying. However, these can be checked and corrected before you have completely finished. One very practical tip I was given many years ago on a study skills course was to make sure my sentences did not go over three lines. Another suggestion is not to exceed twenty-five words. The reasoning behind this is we need mental pauses in order to process information in much the same way we do when listening to speech. Whilst it can feel unnatural and awkward to impose such an arbitrary restriction it does provide a structure, particularly for those who struggle with punctuation. Other tips are to read aloud and put in commas or full stops where you naturally pause.

Clarity

Write clearly and avoid jargon. Even non-fiction writers need a plot or narrative arc on which to hang their story so the reader can keep track of what is going on. Otherwise there is a risk that the reader will end up going backwards and forwards to try to make sense of what is happening. If something jars, seems out of place, or a character suddenly appears that does not obviously fit then there is a real danger of alienating that reader even further. Think about whether you are someone who writes long or short sentences. There is no right or wrong, but it does provoke strong feelings in readers. What is important is whether what you are saying makes sense and can be followed easily.

Conventional advice on writing of any kind is to try not to repeat the same words and phrases. This is why the thesaurus is one of the best-selling books of all time. However, I would suggest it is better to repeat words rather than use something that is unnecessarily complicated. This is because many people simply stop reading when they don't understand something or have to keep looking things up. Equally irritating are phrases that seem designed to either impress or hide a lack of real knowledge. So, if one of your ancestors married by licence or held copyhold land assume your reader knows nothing and explain these in some way.

Vocabulary

The type of vocabulary you use is equally important. Slang and colloquialisms can be grating or quickly go out of date, so are best avoided unless quoting. Personal comments and jokes can irritate readers as do the excessive use of exclamation marks!!!!!

My three times great aunt born into an active church-going family in the 1860s is unlikely to have used swear words. Even slang can be geographically specific and someone will spot it if you get it wrong. Whilst local dialect adds flavour it does need to be used selectively so as not to lose those who might have trouble understanding it. I have an old tape recording of poetry that was written in Yorkshire dialect by a great aunt. From this I selected one poem to quote in full in the family history and added the rest into an appendix.

Clichés, Generalisations and Stereotypes

Clichés, generalisations and stereotypes can provoke violent reactions amongst even the mildest natured person. They exist because they are ready made short cuts which encapsulate common experiences and shared perceptions. You will find books, articles, television programmes and people's everyday speech littered with statements like the 'salt of the earth', 'thick as thieves' and 'they travelled squashed like sardines', or depictions such as a moustached mill owner sexually harassing his female employees.

The problem is that clichés, generalisations and stereotypes are very pervasive. Readers tend to recognise, even if only subconsciously, when they are being preached to, if something is biased. As a result, writers who use them are often viewed as lacking in originality. Even worse, their use can create the impression that the writer only has superficial knowledge and does not really know what they are talking about. For these reasons, clichés, generalisations and stereotypes should be avoided wherever possible. This is not to say you should change who you are, but presenting the alternatives results in a richer more in-depth piece of writing. Moreover, by being original, precise and specific in how you present characters and events you will achieve a rounded and historically correct family history.

Some authors do bring clichés and so on into a narrative in a conscious and 'knowing' manner to give them emphasis and show they are aware of what they are. This can be seen in Lorna Sage's memoir *Bad Blood* in which she uses capitalisation to draw attention to commonly used sayings in her family. Another method is to make a direct reference. For example, 'with his mistress, title and landed estates Roger was the stereotype of a 19th century upper class gentleman'.

Tips
- Think about what you are trying to convey about a person or event. Instead of stating for instance that a migrant's journey meant being squashed like 'sardines in a tin' use an alternative.
- If you are not sure whether you are using clichés and generalisations copy your descriptive phrases and words into an Internet search engine, add 'AND' or the plus sign then 'cliché' or 'stereotype' and see what happens.

Exercise
- Collect up to ten commonly used sayings and note what context they are used in.
- Work out at least one alternative way of saying the same things. Make it as specific to the history you are writing as possible.
- Ask friends and families to list up to three generalisations or clichés they find irritating and tell you why. One of mine is 'little did they

know' as a means of forewarning the reader something momentous will happen, or a flashback to someone's past. The reason I dislike it so much is that it is a self-evident truth and therefore does not need saying, particularly not in the tone of a cheesy over dramatised television voice over. Another is 'hardworking families'; a phrase much beloved by politicians, but one that makes me ask if it means that everyone in every family – children included – works or is working hard. It is also guaranteed to make those who are not in 'families' gnash their teeth and ask 'what about the rest of us?'

- Now find an alternative way of saying the same thing.

Reliability

It is just as important when writing a family history to be rigorous about the quality of the background information you use as in gathering evidence of relationships. Unfortunately, not all historical sources are created equal and there will be times when the information collected simply does not add up. A good written family history will draw attention to research quandaries and problematic source material (often in the foreword or an appendix).

It is equally important to be critical and analytical about family stories, conventional histories, memoires and village histories. Occasionally, this means having to be very diplomatic, especially if your findings and interpretation differ from conventional family lore. When writing one history I was sent copies of letters a family member had written in the 1940s which included all manner of stories and recollections about the family. My problem came with the letter writer's tendency to make sweeping statements about the past, some of which were wildly inaccurate. What I did was include scans of the letters so people can see the originals, and quoted from them extensively within the text. As I wrote about events and the family members mentioned in them I directly addressed any inaccurate statements with phrases like 'although granny Dixon believed . . .', or, 'the evidence contradicts the claim made by granny Dixon'.

Exercise

- Take three or four people from your family tree. Create a mini biography for each person before in the form of bullet points, a family tree or simple sentences.
- Ask yourself whether the narrative keeps moving briskly along. Do you want to know what comes next and are you curious about the circumstances of their lives?

I'm Stuck and Writer's Block

Writer's block is not just confined to fiction writers. It can still be a struggle to put words on paper even when all the information is available. The process of writing is self-generating so one of the most important things is to keep writing regardless of what you think of its quality.

Tips

- Keep your writing time sacred as diverting into doing additional research when the writing is difficult makes it harder to refocus. Instead, use your writing time for reading, collating notes or fact checking.
- Sometimes it is easier to step back and write about a person with whom we are not involved. So try swapping an ancestor with a friend and write about theirs.

Exercise

- Go back to your timeline. Take one fact from it at random and write it up as a single sentence or short paragraph.
- Alternatively, write this fact up into 600 words or 6 sentences.
- Now try and expand this one piece to twice the length.
- Do the same with another fact.
- Keep doing this regardless of how rough the writing is. Once you have spent half your normal writing time doing this see if any of these pieces of writing can be expanded further or slotted into your family history.

Getting stuck on how to describe something is another common problem. Reading your work aloud, even if just to yourself can be helpful as it not only highlights confusing passages and gaps but can trigger solutions. Another tactic is to describe the problem to someone else. For example, 'I don't know how to explain this complicated family relationship', or, 'I think this section on brick-makers is too long and boring'. Then go into specifics as clarifying the problem verbally often leads to a solution.

Tip

- Going for a walk, gardening or other physical activity is a good method for sorting through a writing problem in your head. Keep a notebook with you to record any thoughts that come to you during these activities. I confess that this is slightly more tricky in my preferred activity of swimming, but I do have one in my bag at all times and recommend a water resistant cover. Gadgets such as iPads, iPhones and similar devices work just as well.

Exercise
- Write a skeleton summary of the section you are stuck on as if you were planning a new section. Bullet points or single sentences work best.
- Now note what the exact problem is, i.e. is something in the wrong place, is an explanation over complicated or is there not enough detail and so on.
- Another approach is to give your skeleton to someone else and ask them how they would put it together. Then try out their solution.

It may be that you have discovered that you really do need to do some more research. In which case set a deadline on how much time to spend on the research before you resume writing. If it involves travelling or waiting for documents to arrive by post then use your writing time to focus on another aspect even if it is not chronological. If you do not set defined limits on your diversion and use the space it has created there is a very real danger of finding yourself just researching.

Chapter 4

MAKE IT INTERESTING –
'BRINGING THE PAST TO LIFE'

It is how our ancestors lived, what influenced their actions and how economics, politics or geography shaped their lives and character that turns genealogy into family history. This is what is frequently called 'putting flesh on the bones', or 'context'. By presenting our ancestors lives within a framework of social and local history we enable others to 'see' their characters and experiences in a given time and place. However, this brings up questions of what kind of context, how much, what, where to find it and how to be sure it is relevant and authentic.

Family histories that are little more than long lists of names and dates are dull. Our aim should be to create a bridge across the mass of detail and unanswered questions so that vague, shadowy figures from the past become memorable in the present. Whilst tastes vary enormously certain generalisations can be made about other aspects that might put people off reading a family history. These tend to be historical inaccuracies; contradictory details; unbelievable characterisation, motivations and actions; repetition and information overload.

Tip
- Use as many historical sources as possible as over relying on one such as newspapers makes any history book hard going.

Exercise
- Think about a book, article or text on a website you recently gave up reading because it bored you and list the reasons why.
- Consider what the author could have done differently to keep your interest and list them.
- Tick off any of your ideas that can be applied to your own work.

Repetition, Gaps and Contradictions

Perhaps the greatest problems facing the family historian is what to do about gaps in knowledge, contradictions, anomalies and how to say the same type of thing over and over and over again. Repetition not only applies to types of information, but to events, locations and occupations too. The genealogist is almost unique amongst historical writers in having to resolve what to do with multiple generations of people with similar occupations and similar accounts of them being born, marrying and dying for example.

Tips

- Invest in a dictionary and thesaurus. Online ones are useful, but not as effective as browsing a print version. Once you have looked up a word or phrase look up the alternatives to the alternatives to see if any new ones emerge.
- Create prompt sheets of different ways of saying the same type of thing that you can refer to when needed.
- Every time a repeating event such as a birth occurs check the words and phrases used previously by using word searches and consciously replace it with others.
- There can be a tendency amongst writers to use flowery or convoluted language in order to avoid repetition. Keep your variations as simple as possible in order to prevent the writing becoming stilted, obviously contrived or difficult to follow.

It is not possible to avoid repetition altogether, but you can make it less obvious. The focus should be on making such material stand out in its own right. For example, if you say 'Mary was born in 1818' in one section, then make sure you do not use the same phrasing in the next section. Instead, you might say 'William and Ann's second daughter Mary was born in 1818'. Or, 'by 1818, William and Ann's family had grown to include Mary'. As long as you do not repeat the same phrasing too close together it is safe to use it again at a later stage.

Exercise

- Look at the following phrases and think of another way to say the same thing: a) Peter was born in around 1821; b) Peter's parents are unknown; c) Peter was a widower when he married Mary in 1881; d) Peter died in 1893 and Mary in 1933.
- Choose an ancestor and do the same with a selection of basic facts.

One very effective technique is to collaborate with other people to create different ways of describing common experiences. The following exercises therefore need more than one person. Although they work best person to person, they can easily be adapted to use via email, telephone or online groups.

Exercise

- Choose a type of event that occurs frequently, e.g. marriages.
- Choose a specific example of this type of event from your own family history.
- Outline the details to someone else and ask them to write about it. Agree a word or time limit.
- If they are working on their family history as well, do the same in return for one of their events.
- Compare their version with yours and see if there is anything from their version you can use to make yours different.

Exercise

This exercise works best with more than two people with everyone in the group taking turns.

- Summarise in around a minute an 'I don't know', missing piece or anomaly. For example, 'Cornelius gives his birth place on census returns but no baptism has been found. Only one couple with that surname appears in this parish in this period. I believe he is their son.'
- The other people you are collaborating with must come up with their own way to describe the same problem.
- Write down their descriptions without discussing the finer details or offering potential solutions.
- Pick one of the suggestions made by someone else and write a paragraph starting with that exact statement (no changes).
- A slight variation is to pick one of these alternatives at random.

Anomalies and contradictions exist in many family histories. Often you may never get definite proof because the records don't exist or don't agree. Sometimes an anomaly may only emerge once the writing of a family history is underway. Researching the past also requires being willing to represent truths even if what is uncovered turns out to be shocking. A good family biographer will then integrate such contradictions and any new discoveries into the family history.

Tips

- Keep it brief when presenting contradictions and new discoveries so as not to overwhelm the reader.

- Put lengthy explanations, theories and details of research into an appendix.
- Within the text use phrases such as 'may have', 'could have' and 'it appears' to indicate your beliefs and theories.

Some of the most boring family histories I have read have been little more than lists of facts and what the author does not know. The challenge is to turn that lack of knowledge into something positive without making it up (unless you plan to write a piece of fiction based on your ancestors). If you were to listen to someone describing their family tree you would undoubtedly hear several sentences beginning with 'I don't know'. This means your family history almost certainly has them too and that these 'unknowns' have been transferred onto the page.

One approach is to transform these gaps into a feature. One of my gaps is my maternal grandmother's Panting ancestors. The earliest I know of originated in Gloucestershire in the early 1800s before moving to County Durham. Whilst there may be more to discover, I decided my starting point was to write what I knew without doing any more research and said so in the introduction. I then explored what I know and don't know in more depth in the relevant chapters.

Exercise

- Go through your work and mark every time you use the same phrases when describing an unknown or missing piece. If doing this by hand is too daunting use the word search function on the computer.
- You can make a note of these repetitions in several ways. One is to go through and highlight the repetitions on each page they occur.
  Another is to compile a separate list noting the phrases and pages on which they occur. For example. 'I don't know' on pages 1, 10, 16, 21 etc.
- Now take the phrases that occur most often and come up with three different sentences that say the same thing. For example, saying 'I don't know' about an ancestor's origins could be turned into sentences that include words such as: i) 'a mystery'; ii) 'origins unknown'; or iii) 'appears out of nowhere'.
- The next step is to replace some of your repetitions with these alternates. For example, when writing about a great grandfather my original sentence was 'I don't know anything about Charles Smith Panting before 1911'. Variations could be:
- 'Charles Smith Panting, a man of mystery'.
- 'Charles Smith Panting's origins are unknown'.
- 'Charles Smith Panting first appears, as if out of nowhere, in 1911'.

Another aspect to 'unknowns' is how to convey family stories, theories and speculation. There will always be a point in writing about the past where the author has to speculate or create theories. This is particularly so when it comes to people's emotions, thoughts and motivations. There is nothing wrong with theorising about why a relative did not marry or why and how they came to move from one place or another. However, we can (and I believe we should) make the reader aware of our views and choices in doing so. This can be done explicitly, say in an introduction or conclusion, or more subtly through the use of phrases such as 'perhaps', 'possibly', 'I think', 'it could be' and 'may be'. The key is to make it clear that it is a theory, but anchor it to authentic and credible research.

For instance, I do not know how my great grandmother Belle Marris liked to spend her spare time. In my writing I might therefore say 'we don't know what music or social activities Belle Marris liked'. Instead of this very bald fact I could use the local histories, memoirs and oral histories of other people from her area to reveal the kind of activities she could have taken part in. In this more positive approach I might therefore say something like: 'there were opportunities for Belle to enjoy herself at the music hall theatre in the nearest town, the various church and chapel choirs and at harvest festival dances'.

This type of detail does need to be assessed in terms of whether the subject was likely to have participated. Once she was a married woman with a family, Belle was unlikely to have flitted from one of these social events to another. Her limited spare time would also have been spent differently to a young single person. It is therefore essential to consider how differently men and women and people from different social classes, religions and of different ages spent their time. In doing so it is possible to present a rounded picture of a community with some well-reasoned indications of what your ancestors might have enjoyed.

Another example is Belle's daughter Eleanor (my great aunt) having an illegitimate child. We cannot know that Belle 'must have been furious' unless it was recorded at the time. Instead, it is possible to draw on contemporary accounts, historical research and similar events in the same locality to create a credible account of how such news was generally taken then. In this case I might say: 'It is not known how Eleanor's parents reacted to the news of her pregnancy, but illegitimacy was considered shameful in many areas'. Or, 'I can only imagine the reaction of Eleanor's mother'.

Other ways to present possible reactions might be to make reference to different attitudes to illegitimacy in different areas and time periods by saying something like: 'Perhaps Belle's support for her daughter simply reflected a general tolerance of illegitimacy in their area'. Or, 'It would be very easy with modern eyes to assume Belle was furious, but there is much evidence of illegitimacy being tolerated in rural areas'. In this case I would then make some reference to relevant studies and evidence that support this notion. The key is not to assert something as true just because you believe it is.

Tips

- Provide a summary of where you have speculated, why and what sources you used in your general introduction.
- Integrate speculation into the text by putting yourself into the text as the narrator and using phrases such as 'I imagine', 'it is hard not to wonder' or 'I can picture'.
- If you have strong evidence to support a theory or opinion then try out phrases such as: 'It is clear from the evidence', 'there are strong indications' or 'the evidence leads me to believe'.

Tips

- Asking why people did not do something, as well as why they did, is equally important. Perhaps a daughter remained at home to care for elderly relatives, or a young man didn't join the armed services during conscription because he was in a reserved occupation.
- Don't ignore discrepancies. If the story about your grandmother's elopement or the parentage of your illegitimate great grandfather do not add up then your readers will spot it. Such stories are still part of your history. One way around this is to weave them into the story whilst pointing out the problems.

Exercise

- Find an account of a social activity that took place in the same time period and/or locality as one of your ancestors.
- Use it to describe how that ancestor may have taken part in such an event without actually saying they did and avoiding saying 'I don't know'.

Exercise

- Choose at least two from the following examples and imagine they are scenarios in your own family history.
- Write a sentence or two about each one that presents a theoretical explanation. This might be to suggest possible explanations, list the ways you might find out more or assert your theory is correct.

- Consider how you will explain your reasoning and what evidence will be offered.

Examples
- Two people with the same name were born in the same time period in the same area, either of whom could be your ancestor.
- A woman's maiden name is given on the baptism/birth of a child if no corresponding marriage can be found for the child's parents.
- Your ancestor consistently says they were born in a certain place on census returns but no record for them can be found there.
- The family stories don't match what you find out about a person.
- A will mentions a relative but you cannot find out how they are related.

What if They were Horrible?

It is quite possible that at some point during your writing you discover something that changes what you believe or reveals some unpleasant aspect about an ancestor. A willingness to consider alternate theories and ideas about your history will strengthen your story. This is because you are trying to represent truths about your family and this is not possible if facts and evidence you don't like are simply ignored.

What happens if you do not like or agree with what an ancestor said and did? When researching my Marris family history I discovered a collection of letters in the Lincolnshire Archives written by the brother and nephews of my ancestor Sarah Marris (née Barker) from America between 1853 and 1865. In amongst references to sickness, deaths, worrying about medical bills, work and personal relationships I was faced with how to deal with some of the attitudes and remarks expressed about other nationalities, native Americans and slavery.

It is essential not to hide or reshape the past as such attitudes were as much shaped by their culture and knowledge as ours are today. One method is to present such views without comment. Another is to contrast different points of view from that time. This works particularly well in family histories that include memoir, family stories, lots of quotes or abstracts and transcripts of letters or diaries. A third technique is to comment directly on changes in attitudes and society. In doing so be wary of using the phrases 'they must have felt' and 'they would have'. These immediately cast doubt on what the writer knows. This is because we cannot assert such knowledge as a fact unless it was recorded or witnessed at the time. What we can do in factual accounts is to create theories about people's feelings and actions, but only when supported by evidence from other contemporary sources.

Exercise

- Make a word search for 'must have' and 'would have' and other phrases that assert an unknown as a fact.
- Rewrite each of these to make it clear they are your opinions.

Exercise

- Choose one historical event such as the abolition of slavery, votes for women, changes to the Poor Law system or transportation of criminals that has some relevance to your ancestry.
- Use histories, contemporary fiction or letters and diaries in local archives to present two contrasting points of view of this event.

Did They Know?

It is very easy to ascribe knowledge to our ancestors that they could not have known. Most people did not spend their day-to-day lives with a sense of impending doom in 1913, or plan for economic disaster after the First World War. Neither were people in 1640 somehow aware in advance that England would be a Commonwealth within a few years. You can of course reflect on how certain indications are obvious to us now and mention any predictions or warnings at the time.

Here and following pages: A selection of documents, old postcards and photographs of the kind that can be used to make a family history more visually interesting and add historical context.

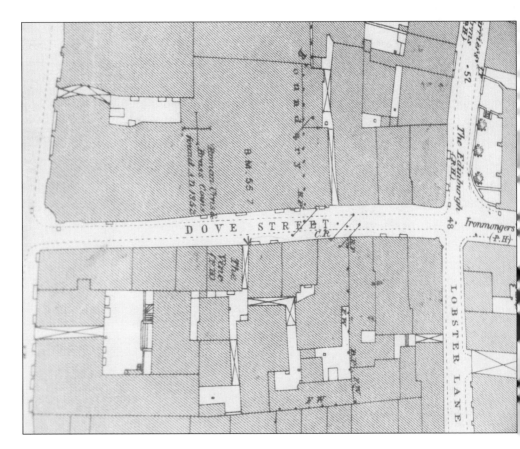

Scotch Girls, Gutting Herrings, at Lowestoft. 1120

One of my students very cleverly discussed diseases and cures in a piece on his family history. Whilst referring to a book on medicine published in the 1700s he pointed out that his ancestors were probably completely unaware of its existence and most likely relied on the tried and tested remedies of the time. Nevertheless, by bringing in published works he was able to draw attention to how traditional remedies were gradually replaced by more formal medical practices. In doing so, he enriched the tale considerably.

Tip
- Illustrate the diversity of past experiences by integrating questions about what your ancestors would have known into your writing. An example is whether someone who lived in the hills of Northumberland would have been aware of the latest fashion craze in London in 1890. Then consider in your writing how long might it take before such information filtered through.

Exercise
- Pick a key national or local event that occurred in the lifetime of one of your ancestors such as the sinking of the *Titanic*.
- Make a bullet point list of what led up to this event.

- Check out how many of those facts were widely known at the time.
- Ask yourself which of these facts your ancestor could have known about and how.
- Consider if the consequences of that event could have influenced how they later viewed what happened beforehand.

Authenticity

Authenticity creates a sense of truth and believability in what you have written. One popular method that helps the reader to connect with the past is known as 'signposting'. This is where reference is made to well-known historical events or people such as the birth of prison reformer Elizabeth Fry or the plague in England. These famous people and events become the signpost to seeing the bigger picture through a sense of familiarity. Another useful technique is to make reference to well-known objects and brand names that people could have used in that era.

All resources require a critical eye. This is particularly true of family stories which change shape as they get retold. In addition to which people's memories are notoriously unreliable. In many cases they are influenced by what has been learnt later, whilst some people are deliberately selective in what they recall. What facts, images and stories we choose to put in a family history can say as much about our own interests as it does about our ancestors. Another point is that you are likely to be representing experiences completely alien to your own. Your readers trust you to represent this accurately.

Guides to research and local history guides frequently include background information. The *Family and Local History Handbook* and *Irish Family and Local History Handbook* by Robert and Elizabeth Blatchford (eds) (www.genealogical.co.uk) are fantastic resources for writers looking for background information. These contain a wide range of articles on different types of documents, occupations and how to research particular aspects. The 2013 issue of the UK version includes articles on newspapers, clandestine burials, turnkeys and wardens for instance. Two articles I found of particular interest were 'British Volunteers in the Spanish Civil War' and 'Sport and Games in the Regency England'.

Despite drawing on historical material it is still possible to get it wrong. Someone farming in the Welsh mountains will have a completely different experience to a farmer in the Cambridgeshire fens, whilst a labourer living in a Cornish fishing village in 1850 may have more in common with Norfolk and Suffolk fishing folk than a labourer working in a Sheffield factory.

One small fact, a phrase or opinion that does not fit in terms of history, geography, class, gender or religion is enough to make a reader doubt everything else that has been written. Many people will be aware of a famous film set in Roman times in which a character was wearing a wrist watch. I could describe numerous similar experiences in family histories from references to births and deaths instead of baptisms and burials in parish registers to the use of slang that belongs quite specifically to a different time period.

Tips

- Creating timelines is a very useful technique to make sure facts, dates and details fit together. A bonus is that timelines can double as illustrations and a means of summarising a mass of information into a digestible format.
- Check and double check historical and genealogical facts. Amongst my favourite guides are *The Oxford Companion to Family and Local History*, edited by David Hey (2nd edn, Oxford University Press, 2010); the *Modern History Sourcebook* at www.fordham.edu/halsall/mod/modsbook20.html and the various local histories and genealogical guides published by Pen and Sword Books (www.pen-and-sword.co.uk).
- Check if a word was in use in a particular time period in the *Oxford Dictionary of Word Origins* (2nd edn, Oxford University Press, 2010) or other dictionaries and histories of words and phrases. Most people can access the online Oxford English Dictionary through their library subscriptions.
- *Handbook of Dates for Students of English History* by C.R. Cheney and Michael Jones (Cambridge University Press, 2000) can be used to check what day of the week an event happened and identify precise dates from documentary references.
- Aim at the intelligent reader who might not know much about what they are reading. If your reader is knowledgeable they will simply absorb that the background is relevant and authentic and carry on reading. Those that don't know much will appreciate the information.

What Historical Context?

Facts are what underpin your family's story, but it is the everyday details of the places, people, circumstances and events that shaped their lives that the reader can connect with. No matter how little you know about their day-to-day lives, thoughts and feelings there will always be some material you can draw on. Even if you have no personal accounts for your ancestors a sense can be conveyed through what has been uncovered during research and other people's accounts. An enthusiastic blending of contemporary and historical accounts on the impact of war, poverty or migration, for example, will grab the reader's attention enough for their own imagination to fill in the gaps. This is not to suggest creating some kind of tabloid style history. Rather, it is to be aware of how a rich mix of reliable and authentic material can colour in the background credibly.

What follows is a closer look at how different resources can be used to add interest to your family history in order that the reader feels like an eyewitness to your family's life. A more comprehensive list of where to find such material can be found in the resources directory.

As well as looking in local archives, libraries and museums consider collecting family stories by interviewing relatives and local people and recording your own memories. Oral history testimony can really bring a book alive. Whether it is a relative's voice or that of someone else from the same area found in a sound archive, this is as close as you can get to directly being there in the past.

Like many others I often bemoaned the fact that I had not interviewed most of my older relatives when they were still alive. Nevertheless, it is possible to record those who are left and supplement their tales with your own and other relatives' recollections. For instance, I do have a copy of the transcripts made from recordings of my great aunt Eleanor in the early 1980s by her son. These include comments about her brother – my grandfather. My mother did not want to be recorded, but was happy to write down some memories in a series of scrappy notes. I subsequently wrote down other family stories I remembered being told over many years. Another kind of personal account is a few genealogical notes written by my partner's grandmother for his father in the 1970s.

Whether or not what is recorded or written is exciting in itself is immaterial. This type of personal testimony creates a sense of emotional connectedness that is hard to replicate through any other means. I could merely use these as a source to say how much my grandfather liked porridge and didn't want to wear long trousers; describe how my mother's Irish family brought peat down from the bog in creels, or that my partner's grandmother passed on the tale of how her own grandmother was widowed when pregnant. This would be interesting, but still one step removed. Instead, by using their own words directly these small snippets make their day-to-day lives 'real'.

Tip
- Scan or photograph your family history notes and include these images as illustrations in the text.

Auntie Eleanor's Memoirs 1902 – 1993

Father worked as horseman for Mr. Yeoman. I loved Yeoman's farm, used to walk there with father's dinner on Saturdays, a lovely can of veg and scotch broth. The stables were just to the left. I never saw any Yeomans or my Aunt Eleanor Blanchard who kept house there.

Mr. Yeoman retired 1910, succeeded by Mr Mrs Beaver. Nobody in the family can remember what happened to my Aunt Eleanor.

Father then took a job with the Rural District Council, working on banks of the River Ouse until 1915 when he took a short-lived job with peppery Widow Wetherell at Priory Farm, Ellerton, where he could not get on with the foreman.

Father used to do work for Mr. Johnstone and his stud of Shire horses stabled at Sycamore House. Mares would be brought there for stud, or sometimes an "Entire Horse" would be taken out, a gay occasion, beautiful horse decorated with ribbons, caddis braid on tail, dancing in the road, ready for Father to "Walk the Entire"<

Father was a good reliable worker, trusted by his employers, but a bad businessman, easy to take advantage of. Father never smoked and never wore a bowler hat. A mild mannered man, a good father

Mother used to show us a fragment of her Wedding Dress, a brown material, threaded with gold thread, silk poplin I think, a substantial material, popular for a long time. Mother admired Horatio Bottomley and Lord Kitchener, felt it keenly when they came to grief.

My parents were caring and never quarrelled. Mother was bright, clever woman, having been Governess for Cranswicks of Hunmanby.

Mother did a lot of shopping by mail order with a firm called Oxendales. Postage was cheap. Selby had shops – Charlie Wetherall Draper at corner of the Crescent and James St. John Wetherall Grocer in Market Place, branches in the villages. James Wetherall sold shoes, cheap but shoddy, we thought, soles made of compressed paper. We were not made to wear hand-me-downs.

2

Mother made our clothes and Father's shirts. Her sewing machine had a flat lid and I remember pulling Fanny round the room in it. Material 6d per yard, cheap.

Mother was a good cook. We set off each morning 8am, well groomed for school, with sandwiches and fruit packed in basket. We left for home 4pm from school. Strong boots were the order of the day, as Wellingtons were unknown. A Cuckoo sang in a poplar tree in a muddy lane at times. Mr. Lister, gardener to old Mr. Tom Jacques, changed the plants in their front garden frequently, which I looked out for on the way home, as well as studying my daily home work, so I only had to write the answers when I got home.

We always had Quaker Oats for breakfast, Ted being crazy about Q.O., asked for it all the time, so Mother had to ask the doctor if it was OK ? Answer, YES.

Recipe for Mother's OAT CAKE 2.4.6.
        2 oz sugar
        4 oz butter
        6 oz Quaker Oats.
Mix to stiff dough, press 1 inch deep into greased tin, put in 180 degrees pre-heated oven, bake 20 minutes.

Mother had three jam pans of different sizes, I expect they would all now be in antique shops. I used to love blackberrying. Mother made the jam mixed with apples, as we ate a lot of pastry and pies for dinner at school and had soup or broth at night.

NEWSPAPERS We only had oil lamps at home, suspended from the ceiling. Mother never read to us, as we learned very quickly at school. I could read fluently when very young and Mother was often cross because I read from the paper on a Sunday, it being rude for a child to read such on a Sunday. Mother bought the SELBY GAZETTE and FAMILY JOURNAL – something in it for young or old, very rough, but popular. THE YORKSHIRE POST was on the go. I cant remember where we got our papers, as there was no shop.

There were no libraries then, and no Wireless until 1924.

OUR EVERARD PIANO probably came from the old Marris home at Owston. Mother played such as THE LOWTHER ARCADE,

Great Aunt Eleanor's memoirs and notes about her childhood from Chris Blanchard.

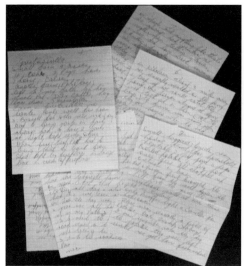

When interviewing people be aware that there are certain ethical issues to consider. You should never record someone without their consent, be prepared to stop if needed and always inform them of what you plan to do with the material. An important guideline for oral history interviewers is to give the interviewee a copy or transcript of the interview and allow them to amend it if they want. Knowing what type of questions to ask and how to encourage an interviewee to open up are skills that take time to develop, so it is worth practising on other people first. Take a notebook and prepare questions or topics to give to them in advance. See the Oral History Society (OHS) for further advice, OHS, c/o Department of History, Royal Holloway, University of London, Egham Hill, Egham TW20 0EX (www.ohs.org.uk).

The range of resources directly relevant to our own ancestry tends to decrease the further back in time we go. One way to overcome this is to present a snapshot of other people they may have lived or associated with. Unless you have a recluse in the family then your ancestors did not live in isolation. Their neighbours, friends, employers, the people with whom they went to religious services, shopkeepers, schoolteachers, the innkeeper and local landowners all had an impact either directly or indirectly. Shining a light onto those people and their neighbourhood can illuminate your own family history. Whilst this is easier if a national figure lived locally there is still a surprising amount of information to be found about less well-known people.

This technique can be seen in the biography of William Shakespeare by Charles Nicholl (*The Lodger*, Penguin, 2007). In it, Nicholl focused on the house Shakespeare was lodging at when he appeared as a witness in a court case in 1612. In doing so Nicholl provides insights to the playwright's everyday life as well as this specific time and place in a very personal manner. He does this by paying attention to Shakespeare's landlord and landlady and the characters that lived and worked there on Silver Street in London.

Diary entries, will excerpts, military records, obituaries and other records offer compelling, first-hand accounts of your family's history. Even if there is nothing written directly by your ancestors you may find mention of them in the records of neighbours and other family members. Include short excerpts within the text of your writing, with source citations to point readers to the original record. Photographs, pedigree charts, maps and other illustrations also add interest to a family history and help break up the writing into manageable chunks for the reader.

We can almost hear ancestral voices in memoirs, songs, folk tales and stories, poetry and oral histories. One family history I wrote for a client includes a history of McAlpine's steel works in Wales because several family members worked there. This section includes a short paragraph on how the harsh working conditions inspired Dominic Behan to write a satirical song in the 1960s called 'McAlpine's Fusiliers' which I quoted part of. As explained in this book, a hod is a device for carrying building materials such as bricks or mortar. It was a pole with a board on, with a second board set at right angles to the first to prevent the load from falling off when the hod was set on the carrier's shoulder.

> No money if you stopped for rain.
> Well, McAlpine's God was a well filled hod,
> Your shoulders cut to bits and seared,
> And woe to he who looked for tea
> With McAlpine's Fusiliers
> If you pride your life, don't join, by Christ,
> With McAlpine's Fusiliers.

In the early 1960s the harsh working conditions were recorded in a ballad written by Dominic Behan, called *McAlpine's Fusiliers*. Though satirical and sarcastic, the song had a strong element of truth and proved very popular. A hod is a device for carrying building materials such as bricks or mortar. It was a pole with a board on, with a second board set at right angles to the first to prevent the load from falling off when the hod was set on the carrier's shoulder.

No money if you stopped for rain.
Well, McAlpine's God was a well filled hod,
Your shoulders cut to bits and seared,
And woe to he who looked for tea
With McAlpine's Fusiliers
if you pride your life, don't join, by Christ,
With McAlpine's Fusiliers.

Work inside the Ebbw Vale Steelworks in the early 20th Century

Page of a family history book showing photographs of McAlpine's steelworks and including a verse from 'McAlpine's Fusiliers'.

For oral history and sound resources check local record offices and family history societies. The British Library sound archives has an enormous collection with some available online via their website. Somerset Archives for instance has some oral histories online (www.somersetvoices.org.uk/people). Old newsreels can be viewed on the British Pathé website (www.britishpathe.com). Films, including documentaries held by British Film Institute (BFI), can be viewed at the BFI in London and their centres in other areas (www.bfi.org.uk). Sample clips can be seen at www.youtube.com/user/BFIfilms. A fabulous collection of folk songs, music and tales including a free online digital archive can be accessed at the English Folk Dance and Song Society (EFDSS), Cecil Sharp House, 2 Regent's Park Road, London NW1 7AY (www.efdss.org). It is also possible to use the huge collections of sound archives that exist in national and local archives such as the one at the Imperial War Museum.

Whilst many family tales and local legends are true, others are distorted, lack credibility or simply cannot be proved. There are a number of such tales in my own family ranging from the likely to the highly improbable. Yet, such tales form a strong part of any family history, if only because of being cherished and passed on. Again, there are a variety of techniques for incorporating family stories and local legends.

Describing the passing on of family tales is the approach I took in writing about a relative who survived the sinking of *Titanic*. I chose to focus on the storytelling process as well as the stories in order to present aspects of the storytellers' characters. It also allowed me to hint at how important oral history and storytelling was in my mother's culture rather than say so explicitly. As can be seen in this brief version I have left room for it to be expanded. If I wished I could also develop this tale to include other survivor's accounts, news reports from the time, public reaction and information on how the tragedy occurred and its wider impact:

'She survived the *Titanic* you know, but would never set foot on a boat again'. The tale of Ellen Glynn's rescue is still told over and over again by my mother's family as if it happened within living memory. The story of how his cousin was helped onto a lifeboat by a young Galway man was passed on to them by my grandfather Patrick Naughton. The family's relief at the time is still almost palpable. Ellen and Patrick never saw each other again, but her letters home and a visit to Ireland by her daughter thirty years later kept the ordeal fresh in her family's minds.

Photographs and objects can act as a springboard for reminiscences or family tales. Memorabilia from the First World War for example is often rich in family lore. If an object has passed down through a family it allows us to tell a much bigger story by focusing on what events it might have witnessed. Edmund de Waal uses this device to great effect in *The Hare With Amber Eyes* (Vintage, 2010) when he follows the trail of 264 Japanese *netsuke* – small wood and ivory carvings – inherited from a great uncle. In doing so, de Waal uses them as a narrative thread by which he explores his family's history. At a less grand level a family memoir by one of my cousin's hinged on the rediscovery of her grandmother's old button tin.

Tips

- Visit locations and local heritage sites. Many tourist sites have lots of information on local history and particular time periods which can be used to show how life changed for your ancestors.
- Let others do the work by watching historical re-enactments to see how people lived on a day-to-day basis.

Here and following pages: Re-enactments of medieval life.

- Take photographs of re-enactors to use as illustrations.
- Check out local museums and their websites.
- Discover the historical material in local record offices and archives. Don't just focus on your own names, check if anyone else from within 5 to 10 miles left diaries or letters, wrote poetry or created artworks. I did this with one history I wrote for a client with ancestors in Needham Market in Suffolk. It has a section on the Crimean War artist Samuel Reed, who was born there in 1816, and a copy of one of his works freely available on Wikimedia (www.wikimedia.org).
- Look at official records from their parish and neighbouring ones such as Poor Law records, wills, histories, fiction, newspapers and journals.
- Don't forget specialist libraries such as the Wellcome Library for medical articles (www.wellcomecollection.org) and the Imperial War Museum for First World War and Second World War related material (www.iwm.org.uk).
- Attend lectures, seek out sound archives and watch quality television shows.

How Much Information?

One of the conflicts in creating an entertaining history is that to write authoritatively requires gaining knowledge, but then having to distil it down. What appears on the page may only be a fraction of what has been learnt. Such paring down is necessary when telling a story in order to keep its momentum going. Yet, it must still give a sense of the additional knowledge underpinning it. When done well this 'light touch' appears effortless and even minimalistic.

In our enthusiasm to create as complete a biography of our ancestry as possible there can be a tendency to include absolutely everything we know. Too much detail can be almost as off putting as too little and technical explanations need care. I once wrote four sides about a set of records that interested me. At which point my 'fierce friend' declared it would be a great cure for insomnia. I had fallen into the trap of putting in everything I knew simply because I knew. After getting over my sulk, I condensed it down to a couple of paragraphs.

One way to include background research without cluttering up the story is to use footnotes, endnotes or an appendix. Another is to include a brief explanation of technical details within the text in brackets. For example, 'William was a cordwainer by occupation (an old term for a shoe-maker)'. If needed, lengthier explanations such as how the term cordwainer was derived from Spanish Cordovian can be followed up in more detail in an appendix. Yet another alternative is to create a stand alone feature within a chapter on a webpage by using sub-headings or information boxes. In this case, I would create one for the history of shoe-making. If the detail takes up more than a quarter of a chapter or webpage then it probably warrants separating out completely into an interlude.

Tips
- Look at family histories, memoirs and biographies that you enjoy and see how they present large amounts of data. Note where and how they go into depth and why that might be. Pay particular attention to any aspects which are mentioned almost in passing yet add to the story.
- Summarise explanations into bullet points or create a list of key points.
- Use charts, diagrams or family trees.
- Imagine you are describing the plot of a short story based around this person or event to someone else.
- Put a very small word limit on each aspect you have to explain.

Exercise
- Take a long or complex description of something you want to explain in your family history. This could be a historical event, family relationships, how machinery worked and so on.
- Write it out in full.

- Now aim to cut each paragraph or sentence in half by condensing that information.
- Consider how else you might convey what is happening through images, personal accounts or contemporary descriptions.
- Aim to intersperse at least one image, contemporary account or other active description into every paragraph.

Does It Work?

Sometimes we can be so keen to include some fascinating snippet we put it in even though it does not really fit. However much time and energy you have devoted to crafting a perfect paragraph, if it does not gel then take it out. This may be painful, but a mass of superfluous text is immensely offputting. Writing comes alive through precise observation rather than vagueness. Choose strong verbs. These are words used to indicate action, an event, state or change. Use nouns (naming words) rather than adjectives (describing words) as these can weaken a piece of text.

Tips

- Always ask if what you are writing adds to the narrative.
- Focus on the specifics of how what you are saying can engage the attention of a reader.

Exercise

- Pick a location and describe it in one paragraph using words of one syllable.
- Now try writing every sentence as a question.
- Rewrite your description into sentences containing five words or fewer.

Exercise

- Turn yourself into your own book reviewer. Interrogate your family biography by asking what is happening on each page and how each paragraph moves the story on.
- Try this first with a book or article you like (preferably genealogy, history, biography or memoir). Do not focus on the content but concentrate on analysing how the author does this. Taking Frank McCourt's autobiographies *Angela's Ashes* and *'Tis* as examples, his writing takes the reader into scenes from the past as if they were happening now.

Adding Context in Practice

A family history becomes truly interesting when we attempt to answer the 'who, what, where, when, why and how' questions.

The less you know about an ancestor the more general background will be needed. This can be done by adding the history of the village, town or city they lived in; describing the landscape; looking up old weather forecasts for days on which significant events occurred; exploring working conditions and recounting tales of local characters. As the author you need to be able to visualise people's actions, characters and beliefs first yourself in order to show them to your audience.

Tips

- Visualise your ancestor in a specific situation such as visiting family, at work, attending church or on honeymoon.
- Can you surmise if it was a happy or sad event?
- Think about the type of place it took place in – house, cottage, one room, mansion or institution?
- Bring in any relatives with them in this situation into the story. For example: 'Thomas Naughton and Bridget Glynn married in 1879, his brother Michael and sister Bridget were there to celebrate and act as witnesses'. This is much more interesting than simply saying 'The witnesses were Michael and Bridget Naughton'.

People's behaviour, choices, and, to a certain extent their characters, are influenced by physical surroundings, the seasons and weather. Describing a street, parish or village where your ancestor lived in relation to its wider environment, their friends, neighbours and employers, breathes life into the page even whilst recognising what has changed over time. Show your reader how people's work and environment changed over time and how work and leisure was affected by the seasons. Let them hear how they sounded by using extracts of people talking in local dialect from oral histories and folk libraries.

Seeing the places our ancestors lived and worked can have a profound impact on our understanding of their lives. In one village I visited I was struck by a very physical reminder of social hierarchies in the past. Walking between the manor house and church at opposite ends of the one original street it was possible to see how these buildings, symbols of power, physically looked down on the rest of the inhabitants. This kind of ancestral tourism is what my daughter and one of her friends nicknamed the 'dead relly hunt' after a family holiday. A word of warning about potential hazards:

The 'dead relly hunt'.

my falling down a fox hole during another 'dead relly' hunt in a graveyard is memorable in its own right.

It is not possible to visit every ancestral area. Even if you can some may bear no resemblance to how they looked 100 or 200 years ago. Nevertheless, we can still recreate a sense of place through the huge amounts of local history resources available in archives, libraries, family history societies and on the Internet. It is however possible to recreate past landscapes from photographs, old postcards, images and maps in particular and blending quotes from diaries, letter, memoirs and oral histories. Some wonderful examples I have drawn on several times are the nineteenth-century reminiscences of the daughter of a Norfolk clergyman who was born in the late eighteenth century. Her grandson has transcribed these and made them freely available on a website along with links to further information on people mentioned in them at www.jjhc.info/joneselizabeth1866diary.htm.

Stories of leisure, food and meal times are highly evocative. One section of a family history I wrote concerned a wartime evacuee's experiences of mealtimes in Essex during the Second World War. The combination of his own words with pictures of an old-fashioned range, foods he mentioned and a couple of war-time recipes from a cookery book triggered a huge response from other people. One of his stories involved his host family paying to use the village baker's oven for their Sunday roast so I added a photograph of the village to show the distance between the bakery and cottage.

Tips

- Use copies of old recipes and household tips and images of now redundant household implements to illustrate day-to-day life.
- A large number of recipe books, household accounts and other related records can be found in record offices and heritage centres; usually amongst estate and personal collections.
- Many old cook books have been republished. Dorothy Hartley's *Food in England* (Piatkus, 2009) is highly recommended. Originally published in 1954, it is full of recipes and cooking traditions from over 200 years.
- Look for cookery related blogs online that focus on traditional recipes.
- Check second-hand bookshops. An old recipe book found in Oxfam was used in the Essex piece mentioned above.

Background detail can be conveyed to the reader in more than one way. When writing about my paternal grandfather Ted Blanchard I could just mention his hobby was restoring old farm machinery and traction engines. A different approach would be to describe seeing him doing so and include pictures of the types of machines he worked on.

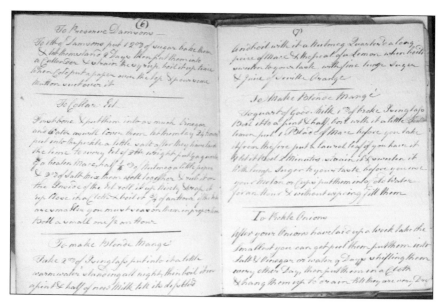

*Here and opposite:
Seaman family recipe
book. (author's collection)*

Meal times then and now.

To expand this further might involve recreating a family visit to a traction engine rally or revisiting one today. As I know very little about farm machinery and traction engines (despite my grandfather's passion for them) I would almost certainly look for books and websites that I could draw on for specific details. In this case, I would also build in details of how my grandfather co-founded the East Yorkshire Farm Machinery Preservation Society, which later became the Yorkshire Museum of Farming at Murton Park. Whilst this involvement is specific to my family, a visit to the same museum would be of use to anyone with agricultural ancestors in Yorkshire. If you do you will see a plaque with my grandfather's name on the wall.

Tips

- Keep a short list of questions you want answers to at the forefront of your mind when writing. Doing so will subconsciously shape your writing towards providing explanations and answers to them. A typical list for me includes 'how did they travel, how did they find

work, who were the people around them and what did they do for entertainment?'
- Draw attention to the things they owned or used that reflect personalities and lifestyle.

Amongst the many contemporary sources that can be drawn on are the letters and diaries of those eighteenth- and nineteenth-century gentlemen who travelled the British Isles in a home-grown version of the grand tour. Often accompanied by sketches, some the best known are the tours of Daniel Defoe in 1722–1723 and Richard Cobbold's 'Rural Rides' across England in 1821–1826. Some of these can be found online, either published by Project Gutenberg (www.gutenberg.org) or on Vision of Britain (www.visionofbritain.org.uk) and British History Online (www.british-history.ac.uk).

One branch of my family originates from Northumberland. In preparation for a trip I looked up local histories. Many feature extracts from the published account of William Hutton, a 78-year-old from Birmingham, who walked alongside Hadrian's Wall in 1800. As he passed within 20 miles of where some of my ancestors lived I used some of his descriptions of the landscape and people he encountered in that area. In addition to which I was able specifically to relate some of his references to what was happening nationally and internationally. See http://en.wikipedia.org/wiki/William _Hutton_(historian) for more on William Hutton and his writings.

Wider context has to be relevant. There is no point in talking about Guardians of the Poor if your ancestor was resident in a parish workhouse in the 1790s. This is because the Guardians of the Poor operated a different system that did not begin until the 1830s. What would be relevant would be to mention the political turmoil that was occurring in Britain and overseas, threats of invasion, wars, fear of revolution and so on. There is no right or wrong way to do this. One way to write about this is to create an interlude in which you can explore that context. Another is merely to mention such events briefly in passing. A third is to link those events to your ancestor's own life, as in this example:

John and his family fell on hard times in 1796 and were forced to approach the parish for poor relief. In one respect John was fortunate. A Poor Law Act the year before authorized the parish overseers to give out relief without imposing the 'workhouse test', temporarily ending a system of deterrence that had started in the 1720s. With a government fearing rebellion amongst the labouring classes due to economic crises and the influence of events in revolutionary France, John and his family were spared that humiliation.

Objects and Images – Writing the Visual

Physical objects, photographs, copies of documents, old postcards, maps, drawings and paintings are immensely powerful tools for a writer. If we are fortunate then there will be some that directly relate to our ancestors. If not, then we can use items from the same time period to reflect on and recreate aspects of our ancestors' lives. Fortunately, there are few places that no one has described, photographed, drawn or painted at some point.

Household objects, personal belongings and work tools are especially effective in drawing a reader into someone's life. We have a piece of camera equipment that belonged to my partner's grandfather, George Seaman Buckingham, a keen amateur photographer who won several prizes and had photographs exhibited here and abroad. There is also an unverified family story that he took photographs whilst in the army during the First World War.

As well as writing about the history of photography generally my biography of him includes a photograph of the camera and copies of some photographs he took that are still in the family. I also explored whether or not the war story might be true and included details of what war

George Seaman Buckingham's camera enlarger.

photography involved at that time. Much of the historical information for this came from the Imperial War Museum, which has a large archive, and the Royal Photographic Society.

Exercise
- Imagine that George Seaman Buckingham was your ancestor and write a paragraph based on the details given here.
- Now take a similar object relating to one of your family members and do the same. If possible, include how they might have used or come by it.

Objects and photographs can tell us much more than can actually be seen. This is because we can recreate certain aspects of our ancestors' lives through interpretation and analysis. For example, I know from my great aunt's memoirs that my grandmother Belle Marris owned a piano, her family used a horse and cart for travel and that she was a very religious woman. From this I can speculate that she probably owned a Bible. I can also infer that she owned knitting needles and sewing kit as the same memoirs mention her making clothes. Also inferred is that the family probably had dogs as they lived on a farm and one is shown in a studio

Belle Blanchard (née Marris).

photograph of Belle. Further inferences might be made about some of the clothes she wore in photographs, family documents and the time period.

Tips

- There is a phenomenal amount of material you can draw on in local record offices, heritage centres, museums, art galleries or as images online. The English Heritage Archive for instance has over 12 million photographs, plans, drawings and records that are free to access (www.englishheritagearchives.org.uk).
- Costume museums, stately homes and art galleries are excellent for finding out about clothes, work tools and household goods. Many paintings and drawings available online have no copyright restrictions on them. For example, when writing about a shoe-maker I found pictures of lathes and other equipment plus descriptions of the work involved on the websites of trade museums (see also the extract from this piece in Chapter 2).

Another technique many writers use when writing around objects,

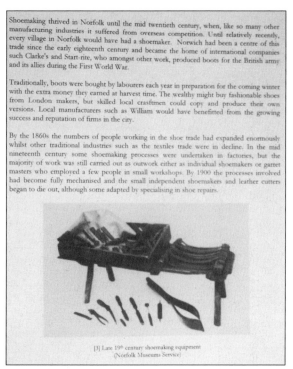

Shoemaking thrived in Norfolk until the mid twentieth century, when, like so many other manufacturing industries it suffered from overseas competition. Until relatively recently, every village in Norfolk would have had a shoemaker. Norwich had been a centre of this trade since the early eighteenth century and became the home of international companies such as Clarke's and Start-rite, who amongst other work, produced boots for the British army and its allies during the First World War.

Traditionally, boots were bought by labourers each year in preparation for the coming winter with the extra money they earned at harvest time. The wealthy might buy fashionable shoes from London makers, but skilled local crasftmen could copy and produce their own versions. Local manufacturers such as William would have benefitted from the growing success and reputation of firms in the city.

By the 1860s the numbers of people working in the shoe trade had expanded enormously whilst other traditional industries such as the textiles trade were in decline. In the mid nineteenth century some shoemaking processes were undertaken in factories, but the majority of work was still carried out as outwork either as individual shoemakers or garret masters who employed a few people in small workshops. By 1900 the processes involved had become fully mechanised and the small independent shoemakers and leather cutters began to die out, although some adapted by specialising in shoe repairs.

[3] Late 19th century shoemaking equipment
(Norfolk Museums Service)

Extract from a family history incorporating an image of a shoe-maker's lathe.

photographs and other images is to blend memoir, facts and stories with a direct commentary on what can be seen. Such a reflective narrative often provides a more direct and personal account. It is one I used when writing a piece about my mother's family and where she lived, as in this short extract.

My mother Biddy Naughton is about 9 or 10 in this photograph, taken in around 1938. She is standing on the right in a pale-coloured shapeless dress, her arm wrapped protectively around my aunt Mary. Sitting with a young Uncle Pat and Aunt Teesie on his lap is Grandpa Pat, who died in 1951. A quiet man, around twelve years older than my grandmother Norah, they were 'matchmaked' by relatives who felt they would be well suited.

Just inside the doorway Norah can be seen peeking out. A tiny woman with bright red hair when young, she was born in 1892, a year before the Gaelic League was formed. Widowed when the youngest of her six children were still in their teens, she continued running the farm well into her eighties.

The Naughton family at Gortavrulla, circa 1938.

Gortavrulla has changed little since my mother grew up there in the 1930s and 1940s. The family farm stands on a steep hill on a narrow lane a couple of miles outside the small market town of Feakle in County Clare. The only neighbours are a few farms scattered over several miles. Long narrow lanes filled with red and purple fuchsia overhang the hedges in summer. We used to snatch the heads off as we rode in the horse and cart to church 3 miles away.

Exercise
- Try using the same technique with a painting, photograph or old postcard that is relevant to your ancestry. Include in your writing a description of where it is, the time of year, what people wore, their hairstyles and physical appearance.
- Compare this to a piece of writing where you have simply added an image without exploring its details. Analyse whether this exploration adds depth to your ancestors lives.

Timelines
Timelines feature in a number of sections in this book because they are such a fantastic multi-purpose tool. As seen elsewhere they can be used for organising your research material, identifying gaps and anomalies and planning your writing project. They are also a means of adding social and local history context, visual reminders of what has gone before and what might follow.

Mini timelines can break up text, reminding readers of complex relationships and as a signpost for what is coming up. Perhaps most of all timelines provide an accessible method of adding social and local history context. Every family and house history I write includes at least one timeline that lists every key event that relates to those people or property. This is integrated with local and national events.

My own method is to create a simple table with three of four columns, although a list format works just as well. One column is for years or groups of years, another is for events relating to that family. Where there is more than one family these might be separated into two separate columns for each line. The other column is for national and local events. Again, this could be split into two if appropriate. Sections of timelines can also be copied and pasted into distinct sections or chapters.

I often start a chapter or new generation of a family with a mini timeline. This will be less detailed than the all-inclusive timeline, but serves as a reminder of relationships and events. This is particularly helpful where there is a lot of information to process, several generations with recurring names and complicated relationships. The following extract from a timeline of the Burlingham family gives an idea of how this can look. The amount of detail included can be expanded or changed as needed.

National and Local Events	Dates	The Burlingham Family
	January 1747/1748	Birth of George Burlingham in Kenninghall, Norfolk to George and Elizabeth Burlingham (née Futter)
	circa 1748	Birth of Margaret Lovick; later the wife of George Burlingham
Horatio Nelson born in Burnham Thorpe, Norfolk	1758	Death of George Burlingham senior in Kenninghall
	1774	Marriage of George Burlingham and Margaret Lovick in Shropham, Norfolk
	1776–1797	12 children born to George and Margaret Burlingham (née Lovick)
America declares independence	1776	Birth of Sarah Burlingham; later the wife of Joseph Seaman Birth of Joseph Seaman in Little Fransham, Norfolk
	1783	Death of Elizabeth Burlingham (née Futter) in Kenninghall
Horatio Nelson created Baron Nelson of the Nile and Burnham Thorpe	1798	Marriage of Sarah Burlingham and Joseph Seaman in Shropham
First national census taken Common lands in Shropham enclosed	1801	

Diary entries, will excerpts, military accounts, obituaries and other records offer compelling, first-hand accounts. Even if your ancestors have left no written words you may find other accounts that mention them or where they lived in the records of neighbours and other family members. At the very least they will supply a first-hand account of the times from someone who was there. See for instance the fascinating glimpses of the seventeenth century in Samuel Pepys' *Diary* which is freely available at www.pepysdiary.com.

Books, books and more books! There is a plethora of histories on every topic imaginable available from the highly academic to the 'then and now' picture-book format. When looking for details of someone who lived in a popular seaside resort in the late nineteenth century for instance I incorporated details from *Holidays in Victorian England* by Gordon Thorburn (Pen & Sword, 2012). See also my book on *Tracing Your House History* (Pen & Sword, 2013) for a wide range of sources for investigating buildings and putting them into their wider context.

Think beyond traditional history books and look for biography, memoir, period fiction, plays and poetry. Quoting songs and mentioning music can also add an authentic feel, particularly if traditional or folk. All of my family histories include verses from songs or quotes from fairy tales and legends. Academic articles and books can be distilled into something more user friendly for a non-academic audience.

Contemporary books, both fiction and factual, can be an amazing resource. If Thomas Hardy or Elizabeth Gaskell already wrote about something of relevance then use their words and insights in your own work (always citing the source of course). Good-quality and well-researched historical fiction written today is often ignored by researchers. If you are fortunate enough to be writing about life in the twelfth and thirteenth centuries, you could do worse than integrate facets from the Cadfael novels by Ellis Peters (a serious historian), which feature a crime-solving monk set against a background compiled from other more traditional historical accounts. The same can be done with any other well-researched and competent historical novelist. Amongst the many that could be recommended are: Jean Plaidy, Bernard Cornwell, Hilary Mantell, Peter Ackroyd, Tracey Chevalier, Mary Renault and Rachel Hore.

Tip

- One useful technique which avoids the risk of plagiarism is to refer to such works directly and include a summary of the events, attitudes and emotions being portrayed in the form of a book report. Try this with a well-known work that has relevance to your own family history such as something by Charles Dickens.

It is not possible to provide a comprehensive listing of the many useful books that can be used. However, a particular recommendation is an excellent book already mentioned. This is *Useful Toil: Autobiographies of Working People from the 1820s to the 1920s,* by John Burnett (ed.) (Penguin, 1974 and Kindle, 2013). Whilst it may not specifically mention the occupation of your ancestor there is an enormous amount of detail on work conditions, training, education and social and political changes in the words of ordinary people.

Another is *The Ragged-Trousered Philanthropists* by Robert Tressell (Oxford World Classics, 2005). This is a fictionalised account of the lives of painters and decorators in Hastings in Sussex in the Edwardian period. First published in 1914, it realistically depicts their poverty stricken lives and working conditions.

Tips

- Browsing library and bookshop shelves can uncover items that would not be found just by searching online.
- Check the bibliographies in books to see if there are any books and articles you might not have thought of otherwise.
- Search the categories of antiquarian and second-hand book listings on ABE Books (www.abebooks.co.uk).
- Check Wikipedia's list of historical novelists at http://en.wikipedia.org/wiki/List_of_historical_novelists and the directory of historical novels at www.historicalnovels.info/ Authors.html.

Convincing background includes sounds, sights and smells. Whilst we may not know exactly what our ancestors wore or the gifts they gave we can get ideas from documentary records. Including small but accurate details from such sources about clothes, hairstyles, transport, manners or customs sets up a scene without overwhelming the reader or misrepresenting the past.

One academic study I have used as a resource for life in a well-to-do seventeenth-century household is *Consumption and Gender in the Early Seventeenth-Century Household: The World of Alice Le Strange* by Jane Whittle and Elizabeth Griffiths (Oxford University Press, 2012). When writing about food I referred to the type of food gifts that Alice recorded in her household accounts between 1613 and 1627. More specifically, I also used the references she made to gifts she received after the births of her children when writing about children born in a similar status household in the same period. Later chapters in the same book provide useful examples of travel and leisure, including the cost of horses and references to a 'jest book' owned by a member of the family and payments to a 'fool' and musicians.

Using such examples works equally well in a compare and contrast format for someone from a different social class. This might be done by pointing out how servants, tenants and neighbours could have still experienced these events. Another might be to provide some examples of life for someone at the other end of the social spectrum.

Exercise

- Pick an ancestor and locate a lifestyle description for someone in the same geographic area and era.
- Locate a lifestyle description for someone in a different social sphere in the same era, and preferably in the same geographical area.
- Write two or three paragraphs comparing and contrasting the different lifestyles and experiences in relation to your ancestor's life.

Newspapers are another fabulous resource. Apart from the possibility of finding a report about an ancestor, they provide local news and views from the 1700s onwards that relate to everybody, whatever their background. If for instance, you find an ancestor died of a particular disease or there was an unusually high number of burials in the parish they lived in during one period then it is worth looking for news of epidemics in the local press. It is however, important to be wary of relying on them too much. Newspapers got information wrong, didn't follow up on stories and reflected editorial bias just as often in the past as today. This means checking any reports found against other sources is vital. If you discover an error or doubt what you have read then consider making this a feature in your writing. For example, in one family history I wrote for a client, I included a commentary on and copies of a death notice, obituary and coroner's inquest report for one man; each of which gave a different age for him.

As well as the local and national press there are a huge number of specialist journals and articles on just about every topic imaginable. Find newspapers and journals at the British Library, at record offices, local history libraries and online. Some of the most accessible are the nineteenth-century newspaper collection on findmypast (www.findmypast.co.uk); the British Newspaper Archive (www.britishnewspaperarchive.co.uk); *The Times* Digital Archive, 1785–1985 (http://gdc.gale.com/products/the-times-digital-archive-1785-1985); and the *London Gazette* and *Edinburgh Gazette* (www.london-gazette.co.uk) and (www.edinburgh-gazette.co.uk). Many of the pay to view sites such as *The Times* can be accessed free via your local library services.

Work and Leisure

After personal relationships and home, people's work is probably the most influential and time-consuming part of their lives. No family history can therefore be complete without exploring what our ancestors did to earn a living, why, where, when and how.

As my Marris ancestors had worked on the land for generations I did not want to keep repeating the same details about agricultural life one chapter after another. I therefore wrote one long section on the history of agricultural work in that region using contemporary accounts and academic and local histories as sources. Part of it went like this:

Life as an agricultural labourer in the eighteenth century involved long hours and little reward. It was common for children as young as 6 to work on the farm; scaring rooks, sorting potatoes or leading the plough horses, with little or no chance of going to school. Wages were low. Any disability or misfortune befalling the wage-earner could result in the whole family becoming destitute. As many labourers lived in cottages tied to their jobs, loss of employment frequently meant the loss of a home as well, with no right to protest.

Then I went on to describe some of the work in more detail. I incorporated quotes such as this one from *The Village Labourer, 1760–1832* by John and Barbara Hammond, first published in 1911 (Nabu Press reproduction, 2012):

Before the enclosure the cottager was a labourer with land, after the enclosure he was a labourer without land . . . families that had lived for centuries in their dales or on their small farms and commons were driven before the torrent.

Another example is for someone with an ancestor in the building trade. I found and used details from this history of plastering and plasterwork to add specific details about the use of urine, beer, eggs and milk to help plaster set (www.deltaconstructionllc.com/history_of_plaster.htm).

The 'what' questions can lead us to the finer detail of people's lives. They most commonly tend to focus on what people did for a living, what they ate and what they wore. In terms of work see *My Ancestor was an Apprentice* (Society of Genealogists, 2010) and *Occupational Sources for Genealogists* (self-published, 1996), both by Stuart Raymond. These guides explore topics that are relevant to everyone. See also the range of research guides published by Pen and Sword books which provide invaluable insights and descriptions into geographical areas, occupations and lifestyles even if you are not sure what an ancestor did.

National and international events that impacted on people's lives are another 'what'. There is always going to be some event that can be linked to an ancestor's life. What makes these outside events interesting are relevance and likely effects. This is where, once again, I use timelines to show what was happening in the same time period someone was born, married or died for instance. Put your ancestor's birth, marriage or death within that timeframe by writing about the probable impact, the after effects or the lead up. This can take a long-term view. National and local newspapers will tell you what was happening nationally and internationally, as well as providing an insight into the prevailing social and political attitudes.

In one piece I wrote I had to include information about an overseer of the parish and how property was passed down through female lines both before and after the Married Women's Property Act of 1882. In the case of the overseer I added an explanation of what their role was and the importance of the parish in local government historically. I used contemporary examples to 'show' my audience how the parish worked by quoting from original parish records, the iconic *Parish Chest* book by W.E. Tate (Phillimore, 1983) and published diaries of clergymen from this era. As the issue of property ownership involved exploring changes in the social and legal position of women I created a separate stand alone section for this. I was then able to refer briefly to such matters in other parts of the history where it was appropriate with short reminder sentences about women's legal position.

'Where' covers where people lived, worked, went to school, fought wars, met married, had children and so on. Many of the same resources can be used, especially as the 'where' in family history often merges with the 'what'.

Tips

- Taking newspapers as an example, check for obituaries, weather forecasts, details of ships arriving at local ports, court cases, the price of goods and other specific local details that you can write into a history to give it a local feel.
- More generally, look out for statistics on epidemics, advertisements for all sorts of goods providing descriptions and prices, or for buying and renting property or hiring servants.

Tips

- Use maps, trade directories and gazetteers to determine exactly where they lived.
- Think about how a place being mountainous, near the sea, in a valley, crossed by rivers or canals affected your ancestors' lives physically.
- Use trade directories to get a potted history of any place in the UK. Available at record offices, local history libraries and online at www.historicaldirectories.org.
- Remember that trade directories and other old histories are often very dated and biased so compare them with more modern versions.
- Wikipedia can be a useful source of information if treated with caution. Do however check who compiled the entries you use and their list of resources used in order to assess their reliability.

Exercise

- Make a copy of a map (old or new) of where an ancestor lived and use this to describe the area.
- Find a newspaper from the week an ancestor was born, baptised, married, died or buried.

A family history featuring a copy of a trade directory.

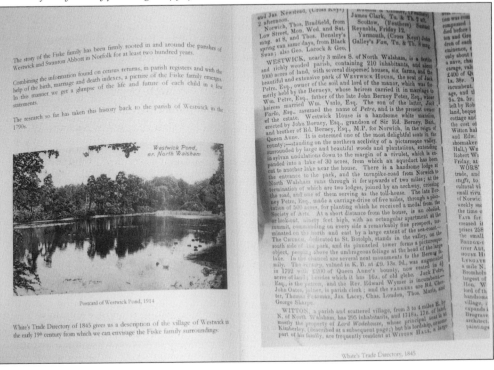

- Choose at least three items from it and include them in the piece you write about that event.

When researching Whickham in County Durham, where one of my great grandmothers was born, I looked at the A Vision of Britain website (www.visionofbritain.org.uk) and GENUKI (www.genuki.org.uk). A vision of Britain includes an extract from John Marius Wilson's 1870–1872 *Imperial Gazetteer of England and Wales* for Whickham. This provided me with a wide range of detail about its physical location and size, employment, population numbers as well as copies of maps and photographs. Included are some writings by Charles Wesley, the founder of Methodism, who had visited the area between 1744 and 1746.

There are a number of ways in which this sort of information could be presented. One is to describe a place an ancestor lived by using these types of information. This might go along the lines of:

Hannah Margaret Ismay was baptised in Whickham in County Durham in 1833. Now a suburb of Gateshead, Whickham had 997 houses in 1851 and a population of just over 900. A decade later, this had risen to just over 1,200.

This might then go on to give a retrospective view of Whickham's earlier history, before moving on to the later period. An alternative would be to write a chronological account by quoting from this source at length. Another variation is to use a range of selective quotes from different sources. For example:

Charles Wesley travelled through this part of County Durham between 1744 and 1746 preaching wherever he could. Writing about his visit to Wickham in 1745, Wesley described how: 'I spake of the length, and breadth, and depth, and height of the love of Christ which passes knowledge'.

Yet another version would be to focus on the history of Methodism first and why Wesley was in area. Or, I might start with the quote then go on to explain why he was there and something about Methodism and Nonconformity.

'At Wickham I spake of the length, and breadth . . .', said Charles Wesley after his visit in 1745.

Tip

- Try comparing and contrasting a place 'then' and 'now' by using such descriptions to show how it was in the past. This could be developed by commenting on what is shown in more contemporary photographs of the area today.

Exercise

- Experiment with putting such descriptions into your own words. First just write a sentence that introduces a quote such as the Wickham example given here.
- Now integrate your chosen quote into a longer paragraph by putting at least some of it into your own words.

Exercise

- Find a description from a contemporary source (including fiction) that is relevant to one of your ancestors. For example, a workhouse or prison scene by Charles Dickens, going to a dance or ministering to the poor in a Jane Austen novel or the travelogue of William Cobbett.
- First summarise the details in order to get a feel for how they express this information.
- Now put the same description or event into your own words briefly.
- Now take your version and expand it further. You can paraphrase and quote sections of the original piece to do this as long as you mention your source.

Exercise

- Pick one event, place or period you want to write about.
- Use trade directories, village histories, etc. from authoritative sources to fill in details of where and how your ancestor lived.

Exercise

- Draw up a list of all the jobs an ancestor had.
- Write down all the places they lived.
- Add a list of people they knew through work or leisure. List how they knew them. Also list any they might have known and the reasons why. Make a biographical summary of the most relevant, interesting or well known of these.
- Note any known hobbies or interests. Also list any that were popular at the time that they might have taken part in.
- Write one to two pages on these facets and relationships (known or speculative). Include your theories as well as known facts.

- At the end assess what, if any, human interest it adds to your ancestor's story.
- If it provides new information, a different aspect to their character or some interesting background context then leave it in.

Exercise

- Choose a subject or aspect from your family history to focus on.
- Decide on an angle – an event; the whole life of person; a geographic area; work; living conditions; personality, etc.
- Think about points you want to make and jot these down in any order – this might be them being poverty stricken, how one branch moved up in the world, the effect of the seasons or impact of particular political events.
- Choose what you think is the best of these points – i.e. the most relevant or the one you keep being drawn to.
- Plan the order you will put these points in – keep in mind impact and put the strongest first.
- Write a first draft – don't worry about style.
- Double-check facts.
- Put it away for a week without looking at it.
- Write second draft.
- Get critical feedback.
- Re-write your piece incorporating at least one suggestion from the feedback.
- Decide it is finished and move onto the next piece.
- Continue crafting your writing until you have completed your history.

Chapter 5

THE NITTY-GRITTY – FROM EDITING, PROOFREADING AND ACKNOWLEDGEMENTS TO COPYRIGHT

A s you move towards finishing your writing there are a number of practical issues to consider. These are editing and revising your work; checking facts and proofreading for mistakes in grammar, punctuation and spelling; where, when and how to use and acknowledge other peoples work; reproducing images and copyright; where to put practical information and making sure people know where you got your information from. Re-working your text to take these things into account can take as long as a first draft.

Editing

A good editor does what I once heard the author Joanna Trollope describe as 'making us the best writers we can be'. Whether it is non fiction or fiction the editor's main task is content analysis; identifying what needs improvement, checking facts and guiding the author to clarify, add or remove aspects in order to ensure that what is written 'works' and makes sense. Although it can be a painful process having your work taken apart in this manner it does result in a better piece of work. This revision process is therefore as creative as the initial burst of writing. An editor may also perform the practical tasks of formatting and correcting spelling and grammar, although commercial publishing companies tend to use different people such as a copy editor and proof editor for these roles.

As the author you are too close to your own work to edit and proofread it. Most family histories are self-published which means organising your own editorial team. Ideally, your editor should have a working knowledge of what genealogical research involves and a grasp of history in order to spot factual errors. The editor's tasks can be minimised if you have shared your work and received feedback throughout its development. Problems to look out for are whether there is enough background detail; unnecessary description; if the point of view (voice) is consistent and whether the events unfolding are logical.

To find a professional editor, copy editor and proofreader see the Society for Editors and Proofreaders, Apsley House, 176 Upper Richmond Road, Putney, London SW15 2SH (www.sfep.org.uk). See also the Society of Authors, 84 Drayton Gardens, London SW10 9SB (www.societyofauthors.org).

There is nothing wrong with using family and friends to keep costs down, but only if they can be truly impartial and have a good grasp of what makes a piece of writing successful. Here are some tips and exercises to try out so that your writing is as print ready as possible before you hand it over to someone else.

Tips

- Check for over-use of the same words. One of mine is 'also'. Many writing style guides suggest 'also' should never appear more than once on a page. My daughter, who often proofreads my work, has been known to order me to make a word search for it, count how many times it occurs and then cut 95 per cent even if I have to rewrite sentences.
- Think carefully about using slang, colloquialisms and uncommon or out of date words, phrases and cultural references. If these really are pertinent to the story then consider if they need explaining.
- Consider varying the length of sentences and paragraphs. Whilst the fashion in writing today is for short, concise sentences, the eye soon gets tired of a standard repeating pattern.

Clarity, Expanding, Cutting and Relevance

It can be hard to let go of something you have written, especially if you spent a great deal of time and effort on it. I can always remember my feeling of outrage to see the words 'how is this relevant' scrawled against a paragraph on my first book. Once I finished gnashing my teeth, I realised my editor was right. I was so busy trying to include a fascinating titbit I had wandered off route.

Tips

- Be absolutely ruthless by constantly asking 'is it relevant?'.
- Deliberately trying to cut 10 per cent from every page will focus your mind on what is absolutely essential to the story and quality of writing.
- Simplify florid writing that has lots of adjectives (describing words).
- Check your explanations are clear and cannot be misunderstood. A

useful method is to give it to someone else without telling them what it applies to. If they can work it out then keep the explanation. Otherwise rewrite and clarify.

- Focus on rewriting one paragraph or page at a time before looking at the whole again.
- Write a section from memory then compare the two versions. This invariably results in a shorter piece and reveals what your subconscious mind thinks is most relevant. You can then merge the best aspects from both.

Exercise

- Rest your work and do not revisit it for at least a couple of days or a week. Then read it again from the beginning. As you do, note the bits you are happy with and tick them off in a bright colour.
- Now, list what it is you like about it such as it flowing well or holding your attention.
- Make a list of anything you particularly don't like and why. Take each one in turn and list three things you could do to improve it. For example, adding an image, finding a contemporary account of a similar event in a local newspaper or a quote from fiction written at that time.

Exercise

- Work backwards through your work to the beginning reading each paragraph in reverse order. This allows your brain to disengage from the content and concentrate on the quality of writing, structure and spelling and grammatical errors. If your work is lengthy do this one chapter at a time.
- As you read, focus on whether the story is engaging; the accuracy of content; clarity of writing and spelling and grammatical errors. Give each paragraph a mark on a scale of one to ten as if you were a reviewer or examiner. See if other people agree with your marking. Anything with a score of less than five needs to be rewritten. Anything with a score of between five and eight would benefit from extra work.
- Make a note of any points you have omitted that need to be included.
- Highlight any sections that have a lot of description and long sentences. See if you can cut these in half by only retaining what is completely relevant.
- Where you have interludes or sections that focus solely on a particular aspect then check these are as concise as possible.
- Once you have made changes read your work again from the beginning.

Exercise

- Ask another writer to rewrite one of your paragraphs in half the number of words without telling them what it is you are trying to convey.
- Look at what elements of your ancestral story they have focused on as the core of this abbreviated version.
- Note the words and phrases they have changed or removed and whether you think they are still essential to your piece.
- Now rewrite their version and see whether any of the words and phrases they removed should go back in.

As mentioned before a timeline is a fantastic genealogical and writing tool. In editing it is an effective proofreading tool with which to cross-check facts, identify gaps and inconsistencies and make sure the chronology hangs together properly. I use timelines to cross-check against the text and can guarantee spotting some discrepancy every time.

Exercise

- Create a timeline if you have not already done so. Cross-check dates and information on it against family trees and documentary resources.
- Read through each chapter or section of your history and add the facts mentioned to the timeline. Include general and local historical events that are relevant to your ancestors.
- Reverse the process and check that the facts listed on your timeline correspond with what is in the text. Use the word search facility on your computer to search for dates and specific words as you do this.

Redrafting and Rewriting

There is no right or wrong way to revise and rework your own writing. It is also not uncommon to produce several drafts before final publication. Some writers edit and redraft after a set number of words, some do it every chapter, at the beginning or end of every writing session, whilst others wait until they have finished a full draft. My own approach is to review, edit and rewrite as I go along. I start by working on individual chapters or sections, labelling each version with a number or date so as not to lose track. Some editing is done on the computer, but I tend to print out hard copies of longer pieces in order to get a proper overview.

I look specifically at how the sentences work and whether anything needs expanding, clarifying or contracting. I make notes and write questions and comments to myself such as 're-phrase, condense, move text, clumsy, rewrite'. Sometimes this results in cutting a good piece of writing because it doesn't fit. If it is a stand alone piece that might be of use in a future piece of work I save it.

The opposite may occur. I once ended up writing an in-depth piece about the design of Liverpool Street railway station. My original piece was about the death of someone after falling down the station stairs in the early 1900s. This was very short until I found references to other accidents. I then added in details about the station design and the trend of commuting from the suburbs in this era as well as relevant accounts from coroners' inquests and newspaper reports.

For me there is an ongoing re-reading and repetition process as I often start to redraft before I have finished a full reading. In the process I add other editorial notes as I type. I either put these notes in square brackets; bold type; capital letters or within the margins in order to avoid confusion. Once I have finished working from my hand-written notes I re-read and check against

Examples of this book being edited.

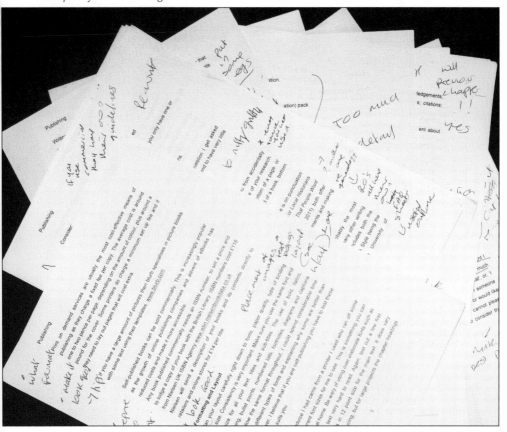

the additional notes made. Then I move onto the next stage of writing and self-editing. Or, I start re-reading again from the beginning to see how it fits in with everything else, obviously making more notes if needed. As a result every page is drafted and re-drafted several times. Once it is close to finished it is handed over to my home team of editors and proofreaders. Then I act on their feedback which involves another round of edits.

Proofreading

Once the content and quality of writing have been edited it is time to proofread one last time for spelling mistakes; grammatical errors; the wrong use of a word; punctuation errors; misplaced capitalisation and inappropriate abbreviations. Proofreading is not the same as reading. When you are reading you may spot an obvious spelling error but not necessarily see other problems. Will you see that the wrong century has been written down? What about the place name or county? Has Sarah Caroline daughter of Sarah Anne accidentally become Sarah Anne daughter of Caroline?

Tips
- Get constructive feedback from your fierce friend. This means being open to other people's ideas and criticisms and abandoning any hint of preciousness over your writing. If you disagree or defend yourself every time your fierce friend makes a suggestion they are unlikely to want to continue.
- Give them clear aims and objectives by listing what you want them to focus on and why. It is no good just giving someone a manuscript and asking them to tell you whether they like it.
- You can get editorial input at any stage of your writing. If you are struggling with a particular chapter or section don't wait until you have finished everything else. Tell other people what you are trying to do with it and how it should fit into the whole and ask them to give you constructive pointers.
- Reading your work out loud is one of the most effective methods of spotting clumsy phrases, an excess of descriptive words or confusing passages.

Exercise
- Here are a couple of examples of clumsy and verbose sentences. First consider the sentence 'he sadly died'. Can you see that whilst someone's death is usually a sad event people don't die in a sad manner? Now think of three different ways of describing someone's death that are more precise yet still convey that emotion.

- Now look at'it was a glorious, bright, hot, sunny, midsummer's day in June'. Clearly there are too many describing words. Whilst we cannot always guarantee a hot sunny day in June it is self-evident that it was midsummer. If it was a sunny summer's day then it was almost certainly hot. If it was'glorious' then do we need to specify it was hot and sunny? Think about how you could improve on this.
- Now check your own descriptions of events and rewrite any that are imprecise or that overdo it.

Grammar, Spelling and Punctuation

Spelling, punctuation and grammar are important because they help our words and sentences make sense, flow and hang together properly. Having said that, being able to explain what a past participle is doesn't make someone good at writing. Grammar, spelling and punctuation are merely practical tools that improve the clarity of the written word. The good news for those that struggle to use these tools is that we are all capable of learning new things. Perhaps even more important is to be aware of your own limitations and to obtain outside help if needed.

The purpose of punctuation is to help the reader follow what you are saying. Short sentences are generally recommended because they make it easier for the reader to make sense of what they are reading. Paragraphs are there so you can put a series of related ideas together. Often they will relate to something in the previous paragraph. Think of them as an expanded list. For example, above are separate paragraphs on spelling and punctuation. Each of these is a series of points or ideas on that one topic. When I started a new topic or expanded on one point within it in more depth I started a new paragraph.

Tips

- Develop a sense of how sentence construction works by copying out passages from other people's writing. The average number of sentences in a paragraph in most books is between three and five. For paragraphs it is around four to six per page. If you have written a sentence that fills a whole paragraph it is almost certainly too long. See if you can break it up into shorter ones by changing a couple of words and adding full stops.
- Check local adult education classes and the Open University for study skills classes aimed at developing the practical use of English.

Perhaps the best known guide to grammar and punctuation in the UK is *Eats, Shoots and Leaves* by Lynn Truss (Profile Books, 2007). There are many companies advertising professional editing and proofreading services in writing magazines and the national press. At the time of writing, a quick check of various companies advertising online found the average charge to be around £6 per 1,000 words for copy-editing and £3.25 for proofreading.

Citation and Copyright

Citing Sources

Always, always, always, always acknowledge your sources. This is not negotiable. One of the biggest frustrations to any reader of family history is to wonder where a piece of information came from and whether it is correct. Source citations are therefore an essential part of any family book. They not only give credibility to your research, but also leave a trail others can follow to verify your findings.

Most genealogists I know have come across family histories that do not explain where their information came from. Others are so vague they might as well not have bothered to try. One local history book I bought a few years ago did have a list of sources. However, this was next to useless as it classified most of them as 'MSS' (an abbreviation for manuscripts) in the British Library. Given the millions of documents the library holds there is no way that anyone could identify what was used from that description.

Equally frustrating are the number of people who put 'Ancestry', findmypast', 'Origins', FamilySearch or other websites as the sources. I cannot emphasise enough that these are not sources. They are just websites that host collections of records, indexes and transcripts. Alternatively, some people simply state they have 'checked all the census' or 'used all the websites'. This means it is impossible to know exactly what has been researched, to check findings and build on research already done.

Apart from the ethics of acknowledging other people's work, citing your sources is the easiest method to make sure you do not inadvertently plagiarise someone else's work. Even better it provides evidence of your research.

In short, although family history is an enjoyable hobby, you should treat your research with the same rigour as any other research. Even if you have been researching for a while it is not too late to start keeping a record of what you have done, or to improve on what you already do.

There is as much guidance on how to cite sources as there is on punctuation and grammar. *Researching and Writing History: A Guide for Local*

Historians by David Dymond (BALH, 2009) and *How To Write History That People Want To Read* by Ann Curthoys and Ann McGrath (Palgrave, 2011) both offer useful advice. A very useful booklet on how to record your sources and findings is *Basic Approach to Keeping Your Family Records* by Ian Swinnerton (2nd edn, FFHS, 1999).

The National Archives (TNA) has an excellent guide to citation conventions at www.nationalarchives.gov.uk/records/citing-documents.htm. A useful article on citing sources from the Board for Certification of Genealogists, USA can be found at www.bcgcertification.org/skillbuilders/ skbld959.html. Purdue OWL is an American website which has a comprehensive guide to citation as well as many other writing related resources such as how to avoid plagiarism. It includes both the American and English conventions with what is called MLA Style being the most applicable (https://owl.english.purdue.edu/owl). The University of Leicester is just one higher education institution offering free guidance at www2.le.ac.uk/offices/ld/resources/writing/writing-resources/ref-bib.

Quotations

It is good practice to quote exactly what you see and make it clear where it came from. If you want to make a comment within a quote then the convention is to use square brackets as these indicate something has been inserted. A common short-hand method where there are peculiarities of spelling or grammar is to use [*sic*], which means what you see is how it appears.

There are some conventions over the placement of long quotations. In general, anything over about 50 words or three lines should be separated out into an indented section after a colon at the end of the preceding sentence. Indenting makes it obvious that something is being quoted. It is therefore not necessary to use speech marks at the beginning and end of the indented quote as is needed with shorter quotes within paragraphs.

Adding Footnotes and Endnotes

How and where you cite your sources will be partly influenced by the style you have adopted for your history. Most academic and historical works use footnotes or endnotes throughout. Footnotes and endnotes have corresponding numbers within the text. These numbers normally go at the end of a sentence or after a quote.

The notes themselves are added by using either the 'Insert' tab on your computer and scrolling down to 'Reference'. By clicking on 'Footnote' you can choose footnotes or endnotes and whether to use roman numerals or letters. Once you click on insert each note is automatically numbered. With footnotes space is automatically provided at the bottom of the page for the corresponding note. With endnotes this space automatically appears at the end of the document. To repeat the same citation, simply copy and paste the footnote number in the appropriate place. These can be edited if needed. If you move text then the footnote will move with it and be renumbered automatically.

The problem is that most family histories are not aimed at an academic audience even though they incorporate research. Using footnotes and endnotes can therefore be too formal for many people's tastes. Another disadvantage is that they can distract from what is written on the page by spoiling the flow of writing. As a result many writers prefer to use endnotes which are placed at either the end of each chapter or at the end of the book. When listed at the end of a publication endnotes are easier to follow if they are grouped under chapter or section headings.

There are many family histories that do not use footnotes or endnotes at all. Many publishers discourage their use completely. Instead the author relies on referencing documents within the text and providing a list of sources used at the end. A popular method in biographies is to cite the sources at the end of a book without any footnote numbering being given in the text. This works by listing the chapter and page numbers, then quoting the first few words of the text being referred to. After that is the source citation and any additional notes the author wants to include. For example, Chapter 4, page number: 'Grandpa Tom who died . . .': family tales by Chris (Biddy) Blanchard, 1960s–2012.

As well as The National Archives guidelines mentioned above all local record offices will tell you what format they want you to use when referencing a document from their collection. When it comes to published material then you need to choose one of the standard referencing formats and stick to it. Some will argue that you must, simply must, put the authors surname first, others will put their first name, then there are the various formats for listing date of publication.

Whichever style of referencing you choose there should still be a separate list of sources searched, places visited and websites used at the end, along with a select bibliography. If in doubt look at some academic books, preferably history as it is the closest to what we do, and copy their format. What is important is that you are telling your audience where you found your information so that, if they chose to, they could go to the same source.

Copyright

If you copy, photograph or reproduce in any form a source that does not belong to you then it is either subject to copyright laws and/or requires permission to do so from the owner or custodian. The rules over what can be quoted, copied and when varies according to whether it is printed material, music, plays, artwork, documents or digital. These rules exist so that people's intellectual or physical ownership of such works is recognised and to protect them from being stolen or misused.

At the most simple level, copyright exists on literary, musical and dramatic publications for seventy years after the death of the author(s). Manuscripts and documents are classified as literary. Crown copyright exists for all documents produced by government bodies for 125 years from the date published. The Internet, filming and digitisation of documents have created particular problems over copyright. For instance, a letter from 1660 might no longer be in copyright but the digitised image of it is.

Whether you have to pay to use material and/or supply a copy of your work in return usually depends on whether it is for educational, commercial or private use. The Copyright Law UK Service has the definitive guide which can be consulted in libraries or at www.copyrightservice.co.uk. Essentially, you can use up to seven words exactly as written by someone else without citing the source. Over that you are allowed to quote short extracts – usually a few lines – from published works and documents without having to ask for permission as long as the source is acknowledged.

The guidelines are to use no more than 10 per cent of the whole work. This is why most authors paraphrase passages or talk about other authors' works rather than quoting extensively. However, simply changing a few words or the odd sentence and passing it off as your own without acknowledging the original inspiration in some way is still plagiarism, i.e. theft.

Using Copies of Documents and Images from Archive Collections

Reproducing copies of official documents such as census returns and birth, marriage and death certificates is not usually a problem if it is for private or educational use.

Most record offices and archive centres have a bad habit of referring to 'copyright' when what they really mean is the right to reproduce copies of documents and other items in their collections. This is because much of their material does not fall under copyright rules due to age. That does not mean you can make copies as you wish or reuse ones you have already paid for. This is because record offices act as the custodians of these records and apply both their own rules and those of individuals and organisations who do own them with regards to allowing access and copies.

In my experience the majority of record offices, The National Archives and others responsible for private collections are generous in allowing people to use material for private use such as a family history and for educational purposes as long as they are acknowledged and sources are cited according to their guidelines. There is often a charge made for commercial use. For all my published books I have had to approach every record office from which I had obtained copies of documents. All except one waived their fee for commercial use in return for a copy of the book. One insisted on three copies, one for each of their branches, even though the images only came from one.

Extras

Appendices
The family history books I write have a full list of sources with document reference numbers and their locations at the end in addition to a bibliography and list of websites used. This is as well as including document references in my captions to images. I also provide an overview of the research undertaken. Sometimes this overview is integrated within the text of the book, particularly if the research was complex. Other times it forms part of a general introduction, or a separate appendix. In fact, appendices including research notes or reports are an ideal way of sharing your findings without bogging down the story.

Indexes
Unless your family history is only a few pages in length, an index is a really important feature. This makes it much easier for the casual reader to find the portions of your book that detail the people in which they are interested. At the very least, try to include a surname index. A place-name index is also useful if your ancestors moved around a lot.

Evidence and Research Findings
Presenting the research you have undertaken is an important part of your family story. In historical works this is normally presented through footnotes or endnotes and a list at the end. Although some readers may not be interested in an exposition of how you got to where you did, there will be some that are. Moreover, it is important for future knowledge and for your research to be taken seriously to include this information. This does not

mean you have to write an extensive report saying I did this, that and the other and found x, y and z. An overview of the steps taken is sufficient.

There are some excellent guides on how to present your evidence, create theories and analyse evidence. See for example, *Nuts and Bolts: Family History Problem Solving through Family Reconstitution Technique* by Andrew Todd (2nd edn, Allen & Todd, 2000) and *Genealogy: Essential Research Methods* by Helen Osborn (Robert Hale, 2012).

Acknowledgements
Thank everyone who has helped and influenced you. Pay particular attention to those who have had made a direct contribution to your work.

Chapter 6

PUBLISHING

By this stage you should have some idea of whether you want to publish a book, booklets, family newsletter, a series of journals, e-Book, website or blog. Publishing refers to electronic, website and blog publishing as well as print. It doesn't have to be expensive or highly technical to produce a family history. At the simplest level all you need is a computer, to decide how to produce it and how much to spend.

Commercial Publishing

It is extremely rare to find family histories published by mainstream publishing companies as opposed to biographies, autobiographies and memoirs. This is because they only commission work that is likely to appeal to lots of readers such as *The Hare with Amber Eyes* by Edmund de Waal (Vintage, 2010) and *Chocolate Wars*, Deborah Cadbury's history of the Cadbury family (Harper Press, 2010). This means that unless you have a famous ancestor, a juicy scandal, use your family history to say something new about a time or place, can connect it to a historically significant event or have turned it into a rollicking piece of fiction you will almost certainly have to self-publish.

If you are determined to reach a commercial audience then you will almost certainly need to find an agent to take you on. Although some small and niche publishers

The self-published Marris and Ismay family history.

accept submissions directly from authors this is becoming increasingly rare. Agents act as conduit between an author and publishing houses, taking an agreed percentage of any advances and earnings in return. This involves negotiating contracts, including navigating the complexities of overseas rights and marketing and publicity. Some are more proactive than others in helping an author develop their work.

The catch-22 is that many agents are only interested in 'proper' authors. Even smaller publishers like Pen and Sword Books have authors on their books that have come to them via agents as well as those who have not. Royalties on commercially published works are typically around 10 per cent, after any advance has been earned in sales. If you have an agent they will take between 10 and 20 per cent of that for their fee. To find an agent and publishers see the list in the *Writers' and Artists' Year Book*, published by Bloomsbury, 50 Bedford Square, London WC1B 3DP (www.writersand artists.co.uk). Also check out the Independent Publishers Guild, PO Box 93, Royston SG8 5GH (www.ipg.uk.com). For general help and advice see the Writers' Guild of Great Britain at www.writersguild.org.uk.

Self-published books are increasingly being sold commercially. The growth of online publishing companies and e-Books has reduced costs and made the whole process more accessible. Many of these companies offer editorial, marketing and sales services too. Such commercially sold books need an ISBN number – a unique identifying number. These are assigned by a group of agencies worldwide.

As has already been mentioned, registering your book with an ISBN means it is a commercial book even if it is only for your personal use. As such, you must give a copy to the British Library within one month and to any other copyright library that requests one. The address is: Legal Deposit Library, Boston Spa, Wetherby LS23 7BY (www.bl.uk/aboutus/stratpolprog/ legaldep). Publishing companies do this automatically, but it is your responsibility to check whether a self-publishing company offers the same service. If they do not, then you must.

The official ISBN agency for the UK is Nielsen UK ISBN (www.isbn. nielsenbookdata.co.uk). Currently, they charge £132 for up to ten numbers. If required, they will send a description of a book and its contents directly to retailers and online stores for an additional fee per title. Most of the commercial publishing companies provide ISBN registration by buying blocks of numbers for resale. The Alliance of Independent Authors (ALLi) is a non-profit, professional association for those who self-publish commercially (http://allianceindependentauthors.org).

Amazon offers a print on demand publishing option with the option of registering an ISBN and selling your print or e-Book on their website. Listings are free although they take a fee from sales (www.amazon.com).

Even authors with publishing contracts need actively to promote their own books. With self-publishing this is even more essential. It is not in the remit of this book to look at marketing in-depth but there is a growing trend to use social media and market books via Facebook (www.facebook.com), blogs, twitter (https://twitter.com), LinkedIn (www.linkedin.com), Google Plus and Pinterest (www.pinterest.com). Listing your book on Amazon and other online retailers will enable it to reach a wider audience through all major Internet search engines.

Self-Publishing for Personal Use

Self-publishing suits family historians who just want to share their work with a select number of people. Despite its growing popularity, there is still a lot of snobbery about self-publishing or 'vanity publishing' as it was traditionally called. There have also been horror stories of people paying thousands of pounds to fraudulent companies for either nothing in return, or very poor quality services. Disreputable vanity publishers can often be identified through implausible claims of turning authors into best sellers and offers of high-percentage royalty payments. Reading the small print usually reveals a myriad of get out clauses and no identifiable market places. One of the most common is that the author has to buy a minimum number of books.

Nevertheless, there are many reputable companies offering services from basic printing and binding to full publication packages including editing, registering an ISBN number and marketing. The difference is that the reputable companies focus is on supplying a product you want rather than spurious promises of fame and fortune. Interestingly, as self-publishing has become more mainstream there have been authors who have successfully used this route to get noticed by 'proper' publishing companies. Others have become commercially successful just through self-publishing. That said, for the family historian it is wise to pick a company for its printing and binding services rather than marketing and publicity.

Tips
- Check out the advice on vanity publishers on Savvy Writers & e-Books online at http://savvybookwriters.wordpress.com/2013/06/07/isbn-numbers-and-how-to-get-one-2.
- Look at forums, blogs and websites which discuss companies selling self-publishing services. See for example, the discussions on Absolute Write Water Cooler, Bewares and Background Checks (www.absolutewrite.com/forums/forumdisplay.php?f=22), blogs on Writer Beware (http://accrispin.blogspot.co.uk) and advice and discussions on Preditors and Editors (http://pred-ed.com).

- *Writers' Forum* magazine and *Writing Magazine* both run regular articles on the pros and cons and pitfalls of self-publishing.

For print books you need to think about whether to print from home, use a print shop or print-on-demand company (either in person or online). Other factors to consider are the type of cover and cover design and paper. The commercial companies all offer some kind of cover service. These can be anything from stapled card, spiral bound and paperback to hardback and leather. Independent binders such as the one I use locally can be found in telephone directories and business listings. There are a number of bookbinding businesses online such as Unibind (www.unibinduk.com).

The Practical Guide to Self-publishing (Barnes & Noble, 2010) by Paul Chiswick describes how to self-publish successfully on a budget. What follows here is some general guidance and tips based on my own experiences and those of students and colleagues who have self-published.

The cheapest, quickest and simplest method is to print your family history on a home printer and have it bound. You can create your own cover using a computer programme such as Photoshop. Royalty free images for print and e-Books can be downloaded from FreeFoto (www.freefoto.com), Image*After (www.imageafter.com) and Free Images (www.freeimages.co.uk).

One benefit of this method is your family history can be saved as a PDF (Portable Document Format) and shared with others via email or a file-sharing site such as Dropbox (www.dropbox.com). Saving as a PDF is particularly helpful if the text file is large as it reduces the file size. PDFs are more difficult to copy (but not impossible) and are compatible with all computer programmes. Finally, it is the format insisted on by most printers and self-publishing organisations. To create a PDF you will need a PDF creation programme. Free downloads are widely available on the Internet.

Many computer programmes have a 'create a PDF' tool button. If not, then it can be created under 'Save As' and selecting 'PDF', or, under the print commands by clicking on 'Print As' and choosing 'Adobe PDF' or whatever other programme you run.

Tip
- Use a laser printer not inkjet so the ink does not run.

The example shown here is a family history I wrote in a Word document and saved as a PDF for a client. It was simply printed out and put into an attractive folder. If binding is required at a later stage it is a simple task to adjust the margins and page layout so that each side of the page has the right amount of space for binding.

Needham Market Post Office on the High Street, 2010

Needham Market originally grew up around and prospered on the wool-combing industry, preparing the fleeces for weaving, although there were also weaving sheds on the town. In 1245 Henry III granted a Market Charter for Needham to Bishop Hugh of Ely. This market probably came to an end with the wool combing trade in the mid fifteenth century when the bubonic plague swept the countryside and isolated Needham. Although the infection was contained by erecting chains at each end of the town it is thought that about two thirds of the population died.

According to local legend "Chainhouse" and "Chainbridge", place names surviving from the time, were sites where the town's sick left (probably in vinegar, meant to sterilise the infection) and people outside left food in return. Local legends also state that the town was so affected that grass took over the deserted streets and the dead were buried in fields in the town, but it is also possible that at first they were taken down the street known today as The Causeway (believed to be corrupted from "The Corpseway") to Barking church for burial.

In 1558, in the reign of Queen Mary, Needham Market had a brush with royal displeasure when Edmund Pole was burned at the stake for his religious beliefs. In 1776 an attempt was made to revive the markets interrupted by the plague, but this was not successful, although the Annual Fair on the feast day of Saints Simon and Jude (28th October) was held in the main street until about 1900.

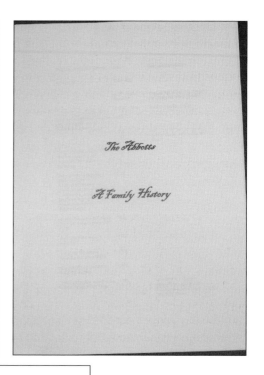

A family history produced in Word, saved as a PDF and printed out at home.

Robert's third marriage took place only a few years before his death. He married a widow called Sophia Cullum by banns on the 27th of September 1872.

Marriage of Robert Abbott to his second wife, Sophia Cullum, widow, 1872

Robert died on the 14th of July 1879. His age was given as 73 on his death certificate, but when he was buried in Mickfield on the 20th of July it was given as 72. He died of heart disease and an inquest was held on the 17th of July. His widow Sophia married again in 1881 to a Samuel Smith. One of the witnesses was Edward Abbott, one of Robert's grandsons.

Death Certificate, Robert Abbott, 1879

Print shops charge an average of 10p to 20p per A4 colour page. The total cost will vary depending on the number of pages, amount of colour and whether it needs laying out, converting to a PDF first or any other preparation. Some printers charge a minimum set-up fee, but it is possible to have a professional looking book of between 150 and 200 A4 pages produced for between £20 and £40 pounds plus binding. The cover is often an additional extra with costs varying according to type and quality. If you have a large number of pictures then Blurb offers a template printing service for picture books accompanied by some text (www.blurb.com).

Print on demand is one of the most cost-effective means of publishing as a fixed fee is charged per copy. The average cost per A4 page is around 10p to 20p, depending on the amount of colour. Covers are extra. Some printers do charge a minimum set up fee and if they need to lay out pages that will cost extra. Many printers and self-publishing companies offer additional services such as design, marketing and retail.

Well-known online self-publishing companies include printondemand worldwide (www.printondemand-worldwide.com) and Authors On Line (www.authorsonline.co.uk). Amazon (www.amazon.com) has already been mentioned for those planning to self-publish commercially. It is also an effective and economical means of publishing privately to distribute to friends and family, with any sales helping towards costs. Other companies offering a range of online publishing packages include YouCaxton (www.youcaxton.co.uk), Matador Publishing (www.troubador.co.uk/matador.asp) and Lulu (www.Lulu.com).

Lulu does not require a minimum number of books to be produced, so is particularly popular amongst family historians who might only want a few copies of their work. What it does have is a minimum number of pages. This is around seventy pages so if your manuscript is less than this I recommend adding photographs to bring it up to the right length. As with many of the other commercial companies they will register your book with an ISBN and sell it via Amazon and Kindle if required. Again, this can be a practical way in which to share costs. The disadvantage (if you consider it one) is that anyone else can buy a copy too.

Tips

- Apart from the legal obligations of giving copies of your book to the British Library and other copyright libraries, sharing your work more widely makes your history more accessible to others.
- Give copies of your book to local record offices, libraries, heritage centres and the Society of Genealogists.

- If you have featured a local church, chapel or other organisation prominently give a copy to the present day incumbents and administrators.

The processes involved with print are much the same whatever company you choose. Authors upload a PDF of their manuscript and any accompanying cover images using their step-by-step guides. Some companies insist on certain fonts and font sizes being used whilst others merely make recommendations. All will tell you what margins to set for printing. If you have not converted it to PDF already then you can be taken through how to do so in the correct manner or they may offer a conversion service for an additional fee.

Using Lulu, it took me around an hour to publish a book from start to finish by following their online guide. This process includes a cost calculator with prices starting from under £5 for a single paperback book of around 80 to 100 pages. What can increase the time involved is reading and understanding their instructions, especially if your file is not exactly as it needs to be. I found some of their guides to solving practical problems such as embedding fonts were not as clear and user friendly as they could be (perhaps because they offer production services for a fee). On this particular point I looked for and found a much more helpful guide at http://lvb.wiwi.hu-berlin.de/doc/embedfonts.pdf.

Looking Good – Formatting and Layout

Whether it is print or online your family history should look good. This is achieved through formatting and layout. If you use a self-publishing company then most, if not all, offer these services as part of a package. So do some local print shops. To achieve the most professional and attractive-looking results you need to plan everything from font size, quality of paper, type of binding to placement of images. For websites and blogs this needs to include how much information you want to present on the home page, the number of links and additional pages and how often to blog and update.

Apart from matters of personal taste, I tend to vary the size of font used for the text according to the dimensions of a book. This is because going up or down a point or two can make a tremendous difference to how it looks overall. Currently, I favour Georgia in 12 point size for the main text, going up a size or two for headings and sub-headings and down one for captions. For smaller projects I find it looks better if the chapter headings and sub-headings are in the same font size.

If you use commercial companies to produce your work then they will have their own guidelines. The fonts used are usually 10 or 12 points in

Times Roman or Aerial for text. Most offer variations in size for headings and captions.

Tips

- A family history book can end up being quite slim despite all the work that has gone into it. Some self-publishing writers like to increase the overall size in order to give a stronger impression of how much work has gone into it. Whilst these are not to everyone's taste, popular methods include increasing the line spacing or creating white space between paragraphs. Another is to use larger fonts. This can have the added benefit of making it easier to read for those with poor eyesight.
- Think about making it easier to read by breaking up long paragraphs into several short ones. This will help retain the readers' attention as well as looking better.
- Be wary of using over elaborate fonts or a very small typeface as these are hard to read.
- Using many different sizes and inconsistency in formatting makes a written work look messy and unprofessional.

Exercise

- Go through your work just looking at fonts and font sizes page by page. Check they are the same for all text, titles and sub-titles.
- Now do the same with the formatting of quotes, footnotes and captions.
- Finally, make the same checks of your use of bold, italics, underlining, bullet points, numbered lists and diagrams.

Text boxes have been mentioned in earlier chapters because they can be a fantastic means of adding extra detail without interrupting the flow of writing. Again, they are not to everyone's taste, and without care, can make a book look odd. I do use text boxes in my own family history books, but for these reasons, very frugally. I find they are a good substitute for footnotes and where an extra notation is needed. For example, the architectural history sections of my house history books often have at least one text box placed on or immediately next to an image. This is so I can include a comment with an arrow that points to a particular feature such as changes in brickwork.

To add a text box using Word click on 'Insert' then 'Text Box' to choose from a range of sizes and shapes. Once the text box is inserted its shape, size and position can be manipulated and there are options to add a coloured background or make other edits by following links under 'Format'

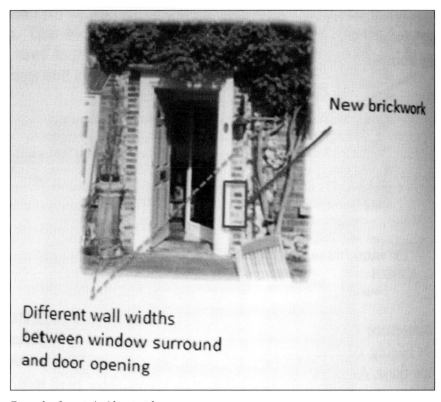

Example of a note inside a text box.

on your tool bar. One major disadvantage to using text boxes is that normal text can get lost underneath a text box. If you are unable to 'fix' a text box in place then think about adding it in after everything else has been formatted. If you do then save the text separately, number it and make a note in your text within square brackets such as [TEXT BOX 1 NEAR HERE].

Tips

- It sounds harsh when said in full, but the best advice is still that well-known acronym 'KISS' – 'keep it simple stupid'.
- Test out different fonts and font sizes on your home printer and compare them with other books and websites.
- Get advice from a print shop, publishing company or bindery on page sizes and margin settings.
- Ask a printer or publishing company for samples before committing to the final print run.
- Make the most of your images by using computer programmes such

as Photoshop (expensive) and Photofiltre (free) to manipulate and edit them. GIMP is another free image-manipulation programme that can be used for image composition (www.gimp.org).

- Experiment with formatting tools in Word to make text flow around images, put extended notes into text boxes and add colour to those.

Layout is not just about looking good. The most important aspects to get right if home printing or at a print shop are the page sizes and margin settings. You must make sure that everything matches up so that the inside pages fit within the cover properly and that the pages look symmetrical once bound. This means that the margins at the top and bottom and sides of each page must be bigger than when printing ordinary documents so that the pages can be cropped to fit.

You can get an idea of the difference by looking at Pen and Sword publications. In general, the overall size of their books is 24cm by 16cm. To make the inside pages fit when cropped the top and bottom margin settings need to be 23cm by 14.75cm.

Open a book and both pages look symmetrical. If you were to remove those pages from their binding you would see that the left- and right-hand edges of each page are not. This is because when a book is bound part of the page is inside the spine. This obviously takes up a little bit more paper on the spine side of the page. This is called the 'gutter' or a 'mirror margin'. So, when you lay out your page you need to make allowances for this. The commonly recommended allowance – depending on how it is to be bound – is between 3mm and 5mm on the edge of the page that fits into the spine. This gutter can be set up within any page-layout programme.

Whilst there is much you can do within a Word document to layout and prepare text and images for print without paying for specialist programmes, these programmes do allow a lot more scope. Such programmes can be expensive unless they are part of a deal with the computer you buy or something you plan to use more than once. Better still are the various free open source software packages, with my own favourite being Open Office Writer at www.openoffice.org.

e-Books

An e-Book (electronic book) can be anything from a single page to hundreds in length. This means it can be used just as easily for newsletters and booklets as a full-length book. Although they are primarily aimed at the commercial market, their versatility in being able to be updated quickly and cheaply has made them increasingly popular with those who self-publish personal projects. Whilst there are some companies only producing e-Books most self-publishing companies offer them in addition to the traditional print format. Kindle is perhaps the best known e-Book format, and it is possible to use Kindle on other devices such as a laptop, tablet, smartphone, iPhone and iPod via a Kindle app (application).

Whilst the same principles apply with regards to making it look good, formatting for electronic publishing does have some differences. This is mainly because of the small screen size of electronic readers. Smashwords (www.smashwords.com) is an e-publishing company that sends books to all online retailers except Amazon. You can use their free style guide to prepare an e-Book for publication regardless of whether or not you use their publishing services. If you do decide to publish via their website they only accept documents in Word as they convert manuscripts to several international formats.

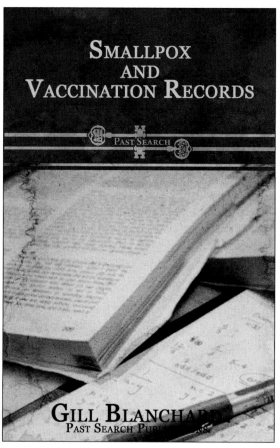

Cover for a Kindle article.

As with print self-publishing, the processes involved in e-publishing are much the same whichever e-Book publisher you choose to use. My first experience of e-publishing was to publish an article, 'Smallpox and Vaccination Records', to Kindle (Past Search Publications, Kindle, 2013). Because it is commercial, it is necessary to register to pay tax and receive royalties on any copies sold. In my experience this is one of the most incomprehensible forms I have ever filled in, but unavoidable.

A very helpful article on publishing to Kindle for genealogists is available free on the website of professional genealogist Geoff Young (www.microgenealogy.co.uk). A further Kindle guide on the same topic can be found for sale on Amazon.

Publishing to Kindle

The first thing to remember is that the traditional layout of books is not geared to electronic publishing. Kindle publications tend to be very text oriented. There are no page numbers and the way it looks on screen will never completely match your format. Although Kindle will structure your work once you have uploaded a file ready to publish there are some ways in which you can make it as good as possible.

Tips

- Using a PDF version means more of your own formatting is retained. When I published my first article to Kindle all the images and captions stayed exactly where I placed them within the text. All that changed was that the text was spread out across a greater number of pages because of the smaller screen size.
- Put no more than a one line break between paragraphs or other text. Anything larger than this results in the white space looking enormous in comparison to a print version of the same work.
- Avoid footnotes as these do not work well, if at all. Instead, put your notes and sources at the end of the document and use hyperlinks within the text to take the reader there.
- Avoid structured data such as tables.
- You can use indentations, bold characters, italics and headings to create basic formatting.
- Manual page breaks can help make a document easier to read and navigate.

The first step to publishing is to set up an account at Kindle Direct Publishing (KDP) at http://kdp.amazon.com or via an existing Amazon account at www.amazon.com.

Once logged into KDP follow the link to 'Bookshelf' then click on 'Add New Title'. The first stage of setting up an e-Book is the marketing section. This is where you describe what it is about, which territories (geographical areas) you want to sell it in, the price and provide your name as author as well as add any other contributors.

You will be asked to upload your file and any cover of your own you want to use. Once all those details are in place you are ready to publish.

The first option is whether to enrol your book in KDP Select. This allows an e-Book to be added to the Kindle Lending Library. Apart from receiving lending fees, e-Books can be promoted via KDP Select by offering it for free for a limited time period. The main disadvantage of KDP Select is that you sign away your right to sell your e-Book anywhere else. This option is only relevant if you are going down the commercial route. Otherwise, choose 'no'.

You will be asked to fill in:

a) Details of publisher.
b) Give a description of the book or article.
c) Add contributors, including your own name as author.
d) Verify your publishing rights.
e) Add categories to promote it.
f) Input keywords – also for promotional purposes.

Having a publisher's name is not compulsory as Kindle Direct Publishing will appear on it automatically if you do not. However, it gives it a more personal feel if you do create your own. Mine are published under my business name as Past Search Publications. The description area is the equivalent of the back cover of a book. This is where people can read an outline of what is in it and something about the author.

Tips

- To make sure you are listed as the author go to 'marketing' in the drop-down menus, then choose 'contributors'. Then add your name. If you are the only contributor then move on to the next phase.
- If you need to add a co-author or other contributor then make sure you put your own name first. It is incredibly difficult to change the details you have put in this section once you go on to next stage.
- This is particularly important if you plan to use your own cover design rather than edit a template from the KDP website. Having not realised that 'contributor' means 'author', I put my graphic designer's name here. Once I moved onto adding a cover it was her name that

appeared on the cover as author. Whatever I tried I could not change this. The only way I found round the problem was to leave the version I had begun as a draft and start again.

There are guidelines in US dollars on what to charge. Currently, anything up to 10 pages should be priced at $1; 20 pages (roughly 5,000 to 10,000 words) should cost $2; 30 pages (about 10,000 to 30,000 words) should cost $3, and so on. The royalties paid are between 35 and 70 per cent depending on the size and price of the book. If it costs less than $2.99 you can only register to collect 35 per cent.

Blogs and Websites

Publishing a family history on a website or blog is a wonderful means of creating family histories that can be adapted and updated at any time. You are still telling a story so need to use all the tools that we have already gone through when discussing how you build a family history that someone will enjoy reading. There are however, some significant aesthetic differences between designing for print and designing for the web and these all relate to the reader's engagement with the medium.

The web can provide a much richer experience for the reader. In addition to graphics you can include sound and video clips and thus make the story more interactive. The web also lends itself to a less linear approach to the flow of the story, with the ability to isolate sections or particular events in a more obvious way. It can help to overcome the problem of how to include additional information without interrupting the narrative flow. As an example, you may have a mass of interesting detail about a person, place or event that is difficult to include without overwhelming the reader. On a web page you could add a link to the information within the text, allowing the reader to choose whether to interrupt the story to find out more, or continue reading and come back later.

Some downsides of web publications are the immediacy of the format and the limitations of viewing large blocks of text on screen. It is always more tiring on the eyes to read from a screen, even a very good one. Reading from a desktop screen requires sitting in a certain place with a certain posture. Although laptops and iPads are portable there are still the issues of balance, the device becoming uncomfortably warm or running out of power. It is difficult to have the same intimacy with the writing and the writer that you get when you 'curl up with a good book'.

Tips
- When publishing on a website or blog edit your family stories into smaller parts to make them easier on the eye and to follow.
- Make it snappy by shortening sentences and adding more images.

A particular advantage is being able to share details of research undertaken, analysis and interpretation of sources and findings in depth. This is in contrast to a book where space and size dictate cost and the inclusion of reports can act as a deterrent to the reader. Research reports and findings, theories and extra background details can be added as separate pages or posts, or as downloadable PDF files. Privacy settings can be used to limit who has access and who can post comments in return. There is no obligation on you to allow anyone else to write and respond.

Websites

This section does not aim to tell you how to design a website as that would take up a whole book in itself. Rather, it aims to show you what needs to be done, options to consider, technologies you can employ and where to go for more help. The majority of the advice has been contributed by my own personal website expert, Ian Buckingham, with some input from me as someone whose first website was set up in 1998.

The first step is choosing where to host your website. There are three main options:

a) Your current Internet Service Provider (ISP) – Virgin, BT Internet, Plus Net or Demon, for example.

b) To choose a company which only supplies web-hosting services such as 1and1 (www.1and1.co.uk) or HostPapa (www.hostpapa.co.uk).

In both these cases you design and submit the website to their servers. All the providers do is rent you the place to put your code. To register a basic dot co dot uk website with a hosting service currently costs a few pounds a year. Additional sub-domains or pages cost extra. Some ISPs do offer free web hosting as part of their Internet and telephone packages.

c) To employ a company that will design the website, submit it on your behalf, obtain the domain and manage its renewal and so on.

Tips
- If you use a company to register a domain on your behalf make sure you own it and/or have full access to it without restrictions. If you do

not, and later stop using that company, you may not be able to access or change anything on your own website.

- Be aware that if you use your current ISP then want to change it later your website could be unavailable during the changeover period.

Choosing a Website Name

When using an Internet Service Provider (ISP) for the hosting service the name of the website includes their ISP name as it becomes one of their sub-domains. For example, if Demon Internet is my ISP and I want a blanchardfamily website and choose the Demon servers as my web host my full website address would be www.blanchardfamily.demon.co.uk.

If, on the other hand, I choose a specialised web-hosting company such as 1and1 or HostPapa I can choose my own website name. In this case it would be blanchardfamily.co.uk. What has happened is that I now own my own domain called blanchardfamily.co.uk as opposed to blanchardfamily. demon.co.uk, which is wholly owned by Demon.

Whilst it is easy to use an Internet Service Provider there are disadvantages in having everything under one company roof. Using the above example, if I did not pay Demon for some reason they would quite reasonably cancel my service. This means I would not only lose my access to the Internet, but my blanchardfamily.demon website too. Having it hosted separately by 1and1 or HostPapa for instance means that losing my home Internet access would have no impact on my website. In this case, the blanchardfamily website would remain available to the world until such time as my domain needs renewing (usually annually or bi-annually).

Most dedicated web hosting companies offer additional services such as free email addresses as part of the domain. This means you can set up email addresses to match your website such as gill@blanchardfamily.co.uk (this is not my real one) or administrator@blanchardfamily.co.uk. Most offer free software as well to help you design and build your website and make it available on their servers. Other optional services that may be available are a newsletter facility, user tracking, and for larger websites, database facilities. This is not to say that traditional ISPs don't offer some of this it is just that offerings from hosting companies tend to be better and more focused.

The end to end solution – a single company that does the design, organises the hosting, website submission, etc. can be attractive if you have no technical skills. The disadvantage is they need to be carefully managed to make sure you do not pay for services you don't want or use.

Tips

- If using a single company, ensure they do not charge vastly inflated fees simply for maintaining and paying the annual re-registration fee for a dot co dot uk domain.
- For anything but the simplest of websites go for the split approach, i.e. separate out the tasks of Internet connectivity from website hosting and website design. It is a little more complex to set up at the beginning, but is far more flexible and reliable. Who knows how popular your site might become?
- Hosting companies tend to be very efficient and fast at resolving technical problems because website hosting is their business. In contrast, ISPs tend to be focused on selling Internet connectivity rather than hosting.

Creating a Website

If you have decided to use your current ISP it should be straightforward. Log on to their home page and you should find a link to 'set up a web site' or 'set up a sub-domain' or similar. If you have a problem, contact their help line.

Follow the instructions. This will include entering the name of your sub-domain, i.e. blanchardfamily, as a sub-domain of Demon. You will be asked if you wish to create any additional email addresses and you may be asked for extra information to do with billing. Take the opportunity to register at least an administrator email address as part of this domain. Once this has been done your sub-domain will become available for use; usually within 24 hours. You should receive instructions on how to upload files to the domain, how to use your new email account and so on. These may appear on the provider's web page, but will more likely be sent by email.

If you use a hosting service such as 1and1 or HostPapa visit their website.

a) On the home page you should find an option to 'register a new domain'.

b) Clicking on this will take you to a page that will ask you what you want the domain to be called.

c) Using our example above we would type in 'blanchardfamily' and then select the type of domain we would like it to be. This is the bit that goes after blanchardfamily in the domain name. In our example it would be the 'dot co dot uk', written using the full stop for the dot.

There are many types of domain to choose from such as 'dot com', 'dot net', 'dot org' and 'dot eu'. The website will then tell you whether or not someone else has already registered this name. If someone has you will not be allowed to continue and will have to choose a different name or suffix.

d) Once you have found an acceptable name and suffix proceed to the registration stage. You will be asked for the names and addresses of the administrative contact and the technical contact. These can be the same person.
e) You will then be asked for payment details and credit card information.
f) Click 'submit' and your new domain will be ready in about 24 hours.

If you choose to use the one-stop-shop option all this will be done by the company you have hired to build your site.

Designing your Website

Now you can start designing your site. There are two ways to approach this. The first is the do-it-yourself approach. The advantage is that you know intimately what you are trying to present, have at least an idea of how it should be presented and knowledge of your intended audience. The downside is you will have to learn to use at least one software package and a certain method of working.

Tips

- Look at the 'Dummies' guides for advice. They are well written and include lots of examples.
- Many design packages come with tutorials and exercises to follow.
- Look around for local courses.

The second approach is to employ a professional or semi-professional website designer. Although professional designers are not cheap they do know the software and techniques and will be able to accomplish things far more quickly than you could. The disadvantage is they may not have any awareness or appreciation of your genealogy and writing, and will thus need a careful eye. A halfway house might be to employ a keen student with computer and web-design expertise.

Layout of Website

There are two main approaches to website layout. The simplest is a single long page which contains the entire book, all the images, etc., usually arranged as chapters. Basically, this is a digital representation of the printed book, but reformatted to appear good on screen. Links within the text can be used to allow the reader to move back and forth or to jump from section to section. This is often the best way for a beginner to start with whilst getting used to what web design can offer.

The alternative is to arrange the text, images and so on as a series of individual pages with links between them. How these pages are divided up and what they contain will depend entirely on how you have planned and arranged your story. It is almost like choreography.

Tips

- Keep each individual page short and to the point, say no more than three screens full of text.
- Adopt a standard layout for each page and stick to it so that the reader's eyes will automatically fall to the correct point when a page is opened. The classic layout is to divide the screen or page into three panels. A short header panel, no more than one-eighth of page depth; a left-hand navigation panel no more than one-quarter of page width, with the rest of the page used for the text.
- Avoid liberal use of bright colours.
- The site should not glare out of the screen because this will make it difficult to read.
- Look at other websites that you like and try and emulate them.
- Seek critical advice from friends and family members and ask them 'can you read and follow this?'.
- Include an index to people, places and events with links that take the reader to them.
- Write a summary of what is on the website and why.
- Tell the public something about you and why you have set up the website.
- Contact details. A personal plea is to give at least an email address and not just use automated contact forms. Such forms create an unnecessary barrier between you and the reader. In addition to which many people simply do not like such forms and they are not always compatible with different web browsers. If you are worried about personal security create an email address that is only linked to this website and separate from your personal one.

Here are some family history websites to look at for ideas on how to present your material and what to include. I have mentioned the website called Reminiscences of Elizabeth Jones (née Helsham), 1801–1866 elsewhere in this book as it is a great social history resource. I include it here because of how it is structured: www.jjhc.info/joneselizabeth1866 diary.htm.

An interesting American example is this chapter from a novel written by Max Terman based on an ancestor involved in the American Civil War: http://clevelandcivilwarroundtable.com/articles/ohio/gettysburg_terman.htm.

Tools

If you engage a designer or use a one-stop-shop company they will have all the tools required. It is worth finding out what they use in case you wish to take over development at a later stage. This brings up a very important point already touched on above in terms of who has ownership and control. You must make sure that, should the developer or company cease trading, you will have ownership of the code for your site. You should also ensure that any domains registered on your behalf will revert to you.

If you decide to design your own site there are a host of software packages available, ranging from the very simple to the extremely complex. Fortunately many of the packages that you would use to lay out a book have the option to output a web page as HTML code. Unless you plan on building a highly sophisticated site with database facilities, user interaction and so on, go for the simplest and cheapest option. Almost all modern design software provides 'what you see is what you get' functionality, so you won't need to get into HTML programming.

A good option to look at is the Serif range of products (www.serif.com) and there are some free, open source products as well. Don't forget that your web-hosting company can help. Many offer a simple template based web-building option, done online, which can greatly speed up the design process, in fact it is easily possible to have a simple site up in less than 5 minutes. Their main disadvantage is that because they are template-based all websites produced this way will tend to look a little samey.

Blogs

Blogs are designed as public forums on which to share news and ideas freely. The word 'blog' derives from 'web-log'. At its most basic level it is essentially a diary that is made publicly available and allows others to comment publicly on what is written. The blog format is ideal for writing a family history even if you don't plan to publish online. This is because it lends itself very well to creating short linked pieces about individuals and events. It also provides a means by which you can reach other people you might be related to or who have ancestors from the same places. As with a website the home page can be found by anyone, but access to other areas can be restricted.

There are numerous guides, courses and workshops on blogging. Genealogist Alec Tritton runs 'Blogging for Family History' workshops at the Society of Genealogists, 14 Charterhouse Buildings, Goswell Road, London EC1M 7BA (www.sog.org.uk). His own blog on the 'History of the Tritton Families' can be found at www.tritton.org.uk.

Fellow Pen and Sword author and genealogist Chris Paton is a prolific blogger both professionally and personally. See in particular his 'Walking in Eternity' mix of history and genealogy at www.walkingineternity.blogspot.com. He recommends looking at Geneabloggers (www.geneabloggers.com) to find blogs on any and every genealogical subject imaginable. Don't forget to list your own with them.

Tips

- Begin your blog post with a descriptive title and brief summary of what it covers.
- Keep it short and simple. The average web user spends only seconds scanning a page to see if it is of interest before either reading more or moving on.
- Even well-educated web users have become used to easily digestible chunks of text so use bullet points and numbered list buttons where appropriate.
- Use headings and body text carefully. You may like the visual look of different sizes and colours, but most readers don't. Perhaps more importantly, neither do search engines.
- Record events and findings as brief notes that can be worked on later. However, do not copy and paste from Word or other word-processing programmes as this can carry over a lot of hidden code that affects formatting. Most modern browsers (Chrome, Safari, Firefox, etc.) have free spell-checker extensions which give confidence when using a browser based page editor.
- Use other people's blogs for information and historical background.
- Add sequels and updates to written work and use it as a means to develop your writing by writing something on it on a regular basis.
- Use it as a means to share information with other family members via email subscriptions, live chats and newsletter registration.
- The immediacy of a blog can be dangerous. As with other forms of social media it is all too easy to post something you later regret. With a family history this is most likely to be a historical inaccuracy rather than exposing your inner self. Nevertheless, once it is in cyberspace, however briefly, someone will see it. Leave a gap and reread everything you write before making it live. If in doubt, get another opinion.

Setting up a Blog

Whilst paying for your own domain name gives you more freedom, most people at least start with a free blogging account. These do have some limitations. The main one is that you do not own the domain name and they can be taken down by the host. Paid for means complete control. The first step is to choose a hosting company, otherwise known as a blogging platform. Two of the best known and simplest to use are Wordpress (www.wordpress.com) and Cpanel (www.t35.com/cPanel-Hosting).

My daughter Cáitlin Blanchard has set up and runs two blogs, including my East Anglian Heritage one at http://eastanglianheritage.wordpress.com. This is from her simple guide to setting up a blog using Wordpress, with some additional input from my website designer, Alex Orton. The set-up is similar on other blogging platforms. Don't worry if you haven't chosen a domain name as yet as you can do later if needed.

Wordpress has been chosen here because it is one of the most popular blogging platforms and has a large community offering advice to new users. Wordpress can also be expanded to create a more commercial site should you wish to. Other blogging publishing sites of note include:

- Blogger (www.blogger.com), run by Google, so integrates well with their other products.
- Tumblr (www.tumblr.com), has an emphasis on picture and video content, so would suit a keen photographer.
- Squarespace (www.squarespace.com), only offers paid for subscriptions, but the money buys some nice features.

1. Visit www.wordpress.com. You will see a screen with a number of options.

- Click on 'Get Started'.

2. Next, you will see a screen with options for your username, password and the web address for your blog.

- Try to use something simple and easy to remember as a blog address, or people won't remember where it lives.
- Remember to use the most secure password you can.
- This is also where you choose whether to use the free www.blogname.wordpress.com option or pay a little extra for a simpler and more professional web address.

3. Wordpress has several packages to offer. The free one is the starting

package, and is the simplest choice. The packages you pay for offer many different things, but I wouldn't suggest them unless you are planning to be a very popular and professional blogger as you won't use most of the things they provide. At this time, I'll walk you through the free option.

- Once you've chosen your blog name, your blog address, and your blog package, all you need to do is hit 'create blog' and you're on your way.

4. On the next page you're asked for your blog title – this is different to the address your blog has, but it is worthwhile making them similar. For example, EastAnglianHeritage.wordpress.com could have the blog title East Anglian Heritage, East Anglian News, East Anglian History, or any number of names you could imagine.

- You are also asked for a tagline. This is just a few words on what your blog is about. Try to keep it to a single sentence. For example: East Anglian history newsbites.
- At this point, Wordpress asks you for a posting goal. If you have one, they email you reminders. If this would be useful to you, go ahead and choose your posting goal. I'd advise starting with one post a week.

5. After you have chosen a theme (see Design section below) you can connect your social networks to Wordpress. If you have Facebook, Twitter, etc., you need to log in to them on a separate browser window now. Then, simply click on the connect links, and everything you blog will be automatically linked on Twitter and Facebook for you.

6. You are now ready to start posting.

Design

Now the fun bit. Do not worry. You do not need to know anything about programming or design. Wordpress conveniently provides you with a collection of pre-made blog themes. You can choose free ones, or you can pay for a special one. It's up to you. Keep in mind these pointers when choosing. It should be:

- Easy to read.
- Easy to navigate (find your way around).
- Look relevant to your blog topic.

There is no limit on the themes you can try out. If you don't like any of the ones they show you, just click 'show more themes', and you'll see more of them. Click on the thumbnail of the theme you like best, and then click next. If the theme doesn't look right to you, don't worry – you can change it later.

When you've clicked on a theme, Wordpress will show you an example of how it might look on your blog. If you like it, click next.

Building Up Your Blog

The Internet has a wealth of expertise on customising and getting the most out of a blogging platform. Putting a description of your problem into a search engine will produce an answer a lot of the time when you get stuck. At first you may have to look up some of the terminology, but soon you should build up an understanding of the basics. When looking to build an audience remember the value of promoting your blog in social media and good old face-to-face conversations. Start-up blogs rarely rank well on search engines, so it's all about getting the message out.

Tips

- Put your blog address and a brief description of it into your email signature.
- Follow other bloggers and ask them to follow you back.
- Make sure any profiles on LinkedIn, Twitter, Pinterest and Google Plus include your blog address.
- Let family history societies and Internet forums know you have a blog.

It is your history, your story. It is time to tell the tale.

DIRECTORY OF USEFUL RESOURCES

This directory is a mix of material referred to in this book and additional useful organisations, websites and publications.

Organisations

Alliance of Independent Authors
c/o The Free Word Centre, 60 Farringdon Road, London EC1R 3GA
http://allianceindependentauthors.org

Arvon Foundation
Free Word Centre, 60 Farringdon Road, London EC1R 3GA
www.arvon.org
Network of writing centres offering residential courses and retreats

British Association for Local History
PO Box, Somersal Herbert, Ashbourne, Derbyshire DE6 5WH
www.balh.co.uk

British Library
96 Euston Road, London NW1 2DB
www.bl.uk

British Library Legal Deposit Library
Boston Spa, Wetherby LS23 7BY
www.bl.uk/aboutus/stratpolprog/legaldep

British Record Society
c/o James Henderson, Rosemount, Riggs Place, Cupar KY15 5JA
www.britishrecordsociety.org

English Folk Dance and Song Society (EFDSS)
Cecil Sharp House, 2 Regent's Park Road, London NW1 7AY
www.efdss.org

English Heritage Archives
Archive Services, The Engine House, Fire Fly Avenue, Swindon SN2 2EH
www.englishheritagearchives.org.uk

Federation of Family History Societies (FFHS)
PO Box 8857, Lutterworth, LE17 9BJ
www.fhhs.org.uk

Imperial War Museums
Lambeth Road, London SE1 6HZ
The Quays, Trafford Wharf Road, Manchester M17 1TZ
Duxford, Cambridgeshire CB22 4QR
www.iwm.org.uk

Independent Publishers Guild
PO Box 93, Royston SG8 5GH
www.ipg.uk.com

Institute of Historical Research
University of London
Senate House, Malet Street, London WC1 7HU
www.history.ac.uk

National Library of Wales
Aberystwyth, Ceredigion, Wales SY23 3BU
www.llgc.org.uk

Nielsen UK ISBN
3rd Floor, Midas House, 62 Goldsworth Road, Woking, Surrey GU21 6LQ
www.isbn.nielsenbookdata.co.uk
Official ISBN agency for the UK

Oral History Society (OHS)
c/o Department of History, Royal Holloway, University of London, Egham
Hill, Egham TW20 0EX
www.ohs.org.uk

Society for Editors and Proofreaders
Apsley House, 176 Upper Richmond Road, Putney, London SW15 2SH
www.sfep.org.uk

Society of Authors
84 Drayton Gardens, London SW10 9SB
www.societyofauthors.org

Society of Genealogists
14 Charterhouse Buildings, Goswell Road, London EC1M 7B
www.sog.org.uk

The National Archives
Ruskin Avenue, Kew, Richmond, Surrey TW9 4DU
www.nationalarchives.gov.uk

UK Copyright Service
4 Tavistock Avenue, Didcot, Oxfordshire OX11 8NA
www.copyrightservice.co.uk

Wellcome Library
183 Euston Road, London NW1 2BE
www.wellcomecollection.org

Writers' and Artists' Year Book
Bloomsbury, 50 Bedford Square, London WC1B 3DP
www.writersandartists.co.uk

Writers' Centre Norwich (WCN)
14 Princes Street, Norwich NR3 1AE
(WCN National Writing Centre opening at Gladstone House, St Giles Street, Norwich in April 2016)
www.writerscentrenorwich.org.uk
National writing centre offering courses, workshops and talks

Writers' Guild of Great Britain
1st Floor, 134 Tooley Street, London SE1 2TU
www.writersguild.org.uk

Yorkshire Museum of Farming
Murton Park, Murton Lane, Murton, York YO19 5UF

Websites

1and1 – www.1and1.co.uk – web-hosting services
ABE Books – www.abebooks.co.uk – umbrella site for antiquarian and
second-hand book sellers

Absolute Write – www.absolutewrite.com/forums/forumdisplay.php?f=22
– discussions on vanity publishing

Amazon – www.amazon.com – booksellers and e-Book publishers

Access to Archives (A2A) – www.nationalarchives.gov.uk/a2a – database of
catalogues contributed by record offices

Alan Godfrey Maps – www.alangodfreymaps.co.uk

Archive CD Books – www.archivecdbooks.org – digitised copies of out of
print antiquarian books

Archive Maps – www.archivemaps.com

Blogger – www.blogger.com – blogging publishing site

Blurb – www.blurb.com – online picture-book printing service

Board for Certification of Genealogists, USA – www.bcgcertification.org/
skillbuilders/skbld959.html – guide to citing sources

British Association for Local History – www.balh.co.uk

British Film Institute – www.bfi.org.uk

British History Online – www.british-history.ac.uk

British Newspaper Archive – www.britishnewspaperarchive.co.uk

British Pathé – www.britishpathe.com – old newsreels

British Record Society – www.britishrecordsociety.org

Cassini Maps – www.cassinimaps.co.uk

Cleveland Civil War Roundtable – http://clevelandcivilwarroundtable.
com/articles/ohio/gettysburg_terman.htm – chapter by Max Terman on
an ancestor involved in the American Civil War

Cpanel – www.t35.com/cPanel-Hosting – blogging platform

Delta Construction – www.deltaconstructionllc.com/history_of_plaster.htm
– includes history of plastering and plasterwork

Dropbox – www.dropbox.com – online file-sharing system

East Anglian Heritage blog – www.eastanglianheritage.wordpress.com

Edinburgh Gazette – www.edinburgh-gazette.co.uk

English Heritage images – www.english-heritage.org.uk/viewfinder

English Heritage and Royal Photographic Society – www.english-
heritage.org.uk/professional/protection/process/national-heritage-list-for
-england

Facebook – www.facebook.com

Family and Community Research Society (FACHRS) – www.fachrs.com

Francis Frith Photographic Archive – www.francisfrith.co.uk

FreeFoto – www.freefoto.com – royalty free images

Free Images – www.freeimages.co.uk – royalty free images

Geneabloggers – www.geneabloggers.com – lists genealogical blogs

GENUKI – www.genuki.org.uk – family and local history umbrella site

GIMP – www.gimp.org – free image-manipulation programme

Heritage Explorer – www.heritage-explorer.co.uk/web/he/default.aspx

Historical Directories – www.historicaldirectories.org

Historical novelists' directory – http://en.wikipedia.org/wiki/List_of_ historical_novelists

Historical novels directory – www.historicalnovels.info/Authors.html

History Pin – www.historypin.com – interactive website

HostPapa – www.hostpapa.co.uk – web-hosting services

Illustrated London News – http://gale.cengage.co.uk/iln

Image*After – www.imageafter.com – royalty free images

Images of England – www.imagesofengland.org.uk

Kindle Direct Publishing (KDP) – http://kdp.amazon.com – see also amazon.com

LinkedIn – www.linkedin.com

Local Histories – www.localhistories.org – lists local groups

London Gazette – www.london-gazette.co.uk

London Lives – www.londonlives.org – free searchable collection of manuscripts from eight archives

Lulu – www.Lulu.com – self-publishing company

Matador Publishing – www.troubador.co.uk/matador.asp – self-publishing

Microgenealogy – www.microgenealogy.co.uk – includes article on 'Publishing to Kindle' by Geoff Young

Modern History Sourcebook – www.fordham.edu/halsall/mod/modsbook 20.html

National Register of Archives – www.nationalarchives.gov.uk/nra – location of archives across the country

National Trust – www.nationaltrust.org.uk

Old Maps – www.old-maps.co.uk

Online Parish Clerk schemes – www.genuki.org.uk/indexes/OPC.html

Open Office – www.openoffice.org – open sources software

Oxford Dictionary of National Biography – www.oxforddnb.com

Parish Chest – www.parishchest.com – publications for sale

Pen and Sword Books – www.pen-and-sword.co.uk – local history publisher

Pepys' *Diary* – www.pepysdiary.com

Phillimore – www.phillimore.co.uk – local history publisher

Pinterest – www.pinterest.com

Preditors and Editors – http://pred-ed.com – advice and discussions on self-publishing

Printondemandworldwide – www.printondemand-worldwide.com

Project Gutenberg – www.gutenberg.org – free e-Books, including old books out of copyright

Purdue OWL – https://owl.english.purdue.edu/owl – comprehensive international guides to citations and avoiding plagiarism

Reminiscences of Elizabeth Jones (née Helsham, 1801–1866) – www.jjhc.info/joneselizabeth1866diary.htm

Savvy Writers & e-Books online – http://savvybookwriters.wordpress.com/2013/06/07/isbn-numbers-and-how-to-get-one-2

Serif – www.serif.com – publishing software products

Smashwords – www.smashwords.com – e-publishing company

Squarespace – www.squarespace.com – blogging publishing site

Sutton Publishing – www.suttonpublishing.co.uk – local history publisher now absorbed into the History Press

The National Archives (TNA) – www.nationalarchives.gov.uk/records/citing-documents.htm – guide to citation conventions

The Times Digital Archives, 1785–1985 – http://gdc.gale.com/products/the-times-digital-archive-1785-1985

Tritton Family History blog – www.tritton.org.uk

Tumblr – www.tumblr.com – blogging publishing site

Twitter – https://twitter.com

Unibind –www.unibinduk.com – online printing and binding company

University of Leicester – www2.le.ac.uk/offices/ld/resources/writing/writing-resources/ref-bib – guidance on citing sources

Victoria County History series – www.victoriacountyhistory.ac.uk

Vision of Britain – www.visionofbritain.org.uk – historical information over 200-year period, including maps and gazetteers

Walking in Eternity blog – www.walkingineternity.blogspot.com

Wattpad – www.wattpad.com http://www.wattpad.com – online writing forum

Ways with Words – www.wayswithwords.co.uk – literature festivals and writing holidays

Wikimedia – www.wikimedia.org – free educational material including images Wikipedia – www.wikipedia.org – free encyclopaedia

William Shakespeare website – www.william-shakespeare.info

Wordpress – www.wordpress.com – blogging platform

Writer Beware – http://accrispin.blogspot.co.uk – blogs on self-publishing and vanity publishing

Writers Forum – www.writersforum.co.uk – links to courses and resources for writers

'Writing Your Family History' courses by Gill Blanchard – www.writingyourfamilyhistory.com

YouCaxton – www.youcaxton.co.uk – self-publishing company

SELECT BIBLIOGRAPHY

Books

Atkinson, Kate. *Behind the Scenes at the Museum*, Black Swan, 1998

Barratt, Nick, *Guide to Your Ancestors' Lives*, Pen and Sword, 2010

Blanchard, Gill. 'Smallpox and Vaccination Records', article on Kindle, 2013

Bristow, Joy. *The Local Historian's Glossary of Words and Terms*, 3rd edn, Countryside Books, 2001

Burnett, John (ed.). *Useful Toil: Autobiographies of Working People from the 1820s to the 1920s*, Penguin, 1974 and Kindle, 2013

Cadbury, Deborah. *Chocolate Wars*, Harper Press, 2010

Cheney, C.R. and Jones, Michael. *Handbook of Dates for Students of English History*, Cambridge University Press, 2000

Chiswick, Paul. *The Practical Guide to Self-publishing*, Barnes & Noble, 2010

Cline, Sally. *Arvon Book of Life Writing*, Methuen, 2010

Cline, Sally and Gillies, Midge. *The Arvon Book of Literary Non-Fiction*, Bloomsbury, 2012

Curthoys, Ann and McGrath, Ann. *How to Write History that People Want to Read*, Palgrave Macmillan, 2011

de Waal, Edmund. *The Hare with Amber Eyes*, Vintage, 2010

Dymond, David. *Researching and Writing History: A Guide for Local Historians*, BALH, 2009

Flint, M.F., Fitzpatrick, N. and Thorne, C. *A User's Guide to Copyright*, 5th edn, Butterworths, 2004

France, Peter and St Clair, William. *Mapping Lives*, Oxford University Press, 2002

Gillies, Midge. *Writing Lives: Literary Biography*, Cambridge University Press, 2009

Hammond, Barbara and John. *The Village Labourer, 1760–1832*, Nabu Press, reproduction, 2012

Hardy, Jeremy. *My Family and other Animals: Adventures in Genealogy*, Ebury Press, 2010

Hartley, Dorothy. *Food in England: A Complete Guide to the Food that Makes Us Who We Are*, Piatkus, 2009

Heilbrun, Carolyn G. *Writing a Woman's Life*, Ballantine Books, 1988

Hey, David. *The Oxford Companion to Family and Local History*, 2nd edn, Oxford University Press, 2010

Hines, John. *The Way to Write Non-Fiction*, Elm Tree Books, 1990

Hoffman, Ann. *Research for Writers* (Writing Handbook), A. & C. Black, 1999

Hughes, Kathryn. *The Short Life & Long Times of Mrs Beeton*, Fourth Estate, 2005

Lee, Hermione. *Biography: A Very Short Introduction*, Oxford University Press, 2009

Lowenthal, David. *The Past is a Foreign Country*, Cambridge University Press, 1995

McCourt, Frank. *Angela's Ashes*, Harper Perennial, 2005

McCourt, Frank. *'Tis: A Memoir*, Harper Perennial, 2005

Martin, Rhona. *Writing Historical Fiction*, 2nd edn, A. & C. Black, 1995

Matthews, Richard. *Robert Toppes Medieval Mercer of Norwich*, Norfolk and Norwich Heritage Trust, 2013

May, Stephen. *Teach Yourself Creative Writing*, in association with ARVON, 2008

Nicholl, Charles. *The Lodger: Shakespeare on Silver Street*, Penguin, 2007

Osborn, Helen. *Genealogy: Essential Research Methods*, Robert Hale, 2012

Phythian, B.A. *Teach Yourself English Grammar*, Hodder & Stoughton, rev. edn, 2003

Raymond, Stuart. *My Ancestor was an Apprentice*, Society of Genealogists, 2012

Raymond, Stuart. *Occupational Sources for Genealogists*, self-published, 1996

Richardson, John, *The Local Historian's Encyclopaedia*, Historical Publications, 1974

Ritter, Robert (ed.). *The Oxford Guide to Style*, OUP, 2005

Sage, Lorna. *Bad Blood*, Fourth Estate, 2000

Steedman, Carolyn. *Past Tenses: Essays on Writing Autobiography and History*, Rivers Oram, 1992

Stein, Gertrude. *How To Write*, Dover, 1975

Swinnerton, Ian. *Basic Approach to Keeping Your Family Records*, 2nd edn, FFHS, 1999

Tate, W.E. *The Parish Chest*, 3rd edn, Phillimore, 1983

Thorburn, Gordon. *Holidays in Victorian England*, Pen & Sword, 2012

Titford, John. *Writing up Your Family History*, Countryside Books, 2003, Kindle version, 2011

Todd, Andrew. *Nuts and Bolts: Family History Problem Solving through Family Reconstitution Technique*, 2nd edn, Allen & Todd, 2000

Tressell, Robert. *The Ragged-Trousered Philanthropists*, Oxford World Classics, 2005

Truss, Lynne. *Eats, Shoots and Leaves: The Zero Tolerance Approach to Punctuation*, Profile, 2007

Waller, Maureen. *The English Marriage*, John Murray, 2010

Wells, Gordon. *How to Write Non-Fiction Books*, Writer's Workshop, 1999

Whittle, Jane and Griffiths, Elizabeth. *Consumption and Gender in the Early Seventeenth-Century Household: The World of Alice Le Strange*, Oxford University Press, 2012

Yorke, T. *Tracing the History of Villages*, Countryside Books, 2001

Magazines and Journals

BBC History Magazine – www.historyextra.com

Bookseller magazine (UK) – www.thebookseller.com

Family and Local History Handbook (Robert and Elizabeth Blatchford (eds)) – www.genealogical.co.uk/index.html

History Today – www.historytoday.com

London Review of Books – www.lrb.co.uk

Times Literary Supplement – www.the-tls.co.uk

Writers' and Artists' Yearbook – www.writersandartists.co.uk

Writing Forum magazine – www.writers-forum.com

Writing Magazine – www.writers-online.co.uk

INDEX